THE REAL WEED MAN
PORTRAIT OF CANADIAN BOTANIST GERALD A. MULLIGAN

JULIE MULLIGAN

P.O. Box 304, Russell, Ontario, Canada, K4R 1E1
Website: http://www.weedscanada.ca

Library and Archives Canada Cataloguing in Publication

Mulligan, Julie, author
    The real weed man: portrait of Canadian botanist Gerald A. Mulligan / Julie Mulligan.

ISBN 978-0-9937698-0-1

    1. Mulligan, Gerald A., 1928-. 2. Botanists--Canada--Biography. I. Title.

QK31.M85M85 2014   580.971092   C2014-903322-2

Cover photograph by Julie Mulligan, Gerald A. Mulligan botanizing on Mt. Charles Stewart, Canmore Alberta, July 2012
Interior photographs: Gerald A. Mulligan
Copy Editor: Ruth Bradley-St-Cyr
Cover Design: Accurate Design
Formatting: Iron Horse Formatting

Dedicated to my father, a person who has had a profoundly positive impact on many lives, including my own

TABLE OF CONTENTS

INTRODUCTION

The idea for this book stemmed from an incident in 2010 at the University of British Columbia, Kelowna Campus. My niece, Robyn Mulligan, was studying anthropology. At the end of a class for which she had been a guest lecturer, the professor posted the students' next research assignment. The assignment was to investigate one of a list of important Canadian botanists, the plants they discovered, their personal background, the region they worked in, their academic background, professional affiliations, and the significance of the person and/or their findings. Gerald A. Mulligan was one of nine botanists listed.

A friend of Robyn's taking the class, piped up, "Hey Robyn, your last name is Mulligan. Do you know Gerald A. Mulligan?" It took a minute for it to sink in, then with great excitement she stated, "Yes! It's my grandfather." Robyn says, "I called Dad right after and said, guess what?"

For a while now, I have wanted to try my hand at writing a book. In the mid-1990s, I investigated writing a biography about one of my former bosses, Macklin Hancock, a celebrated urban planner. He had agreed to the proposal, but with us each living in different cities, it just never worked out. So when I heard Robyn's story, it jarred me into realizing that I had the perfect candidate right on my doorstep. Sometimes you are so close to someone you forget his importance in the wider world.

This undertaking was greatly enriched by the fact that my father has diligently kept a daily diary since 1974. Not only did this add an extra level of detail, but it corroborated my father's phenomenal memory about the events of his life. It gave a lot of credence to memories dating back to early in his life and career.

My father is clear in stating, "The diaries were never an outlet for what bothered me. I have always had to work at keeping the diary. It was not something I felt compelled to do. One of the things that I always enjoyed was seeing what happened at a similar time in the year before, or two years before. I often included little details about the weather or what was in flower. It was interesting to compare. But make no mistake it is a pain to write in it every day! Sometimes, at the time, when I write something, it doesn't mean anything significant, but several years later, when I look back on it, it does. The entries got longer as time went on. They got longer because I found it valuable to look back, and so I started to make an effort to record more information. I always did it purely for my own personal interest." Maybe so, but they have also provided me with a valuable source of information.

I would like to thank my entire family for their support for this endeavour, particularly their frank and often detailed memories and opinions. In particular, I thank my father and mother for sitting through over twenty interviews, and my niece Robyn for sharing so openly her experiences and feelings about stuttering. I would also like to thank my father's friends, and former and current colleagues for their input and perspectives.

1
THE EARLY YEARS

My great-grandfather Alexander was the second generation of the Mulligan family in Canada to marry a French-Canadian. Alex, as he was known, married Matilda Blondin and had eleven children. Wilfred, the second oldest, was my grandfather, born in Ottawa in 1896. Wilfred was brought up speaking French as his first language. He attended St-Jean-Baptiste French School to grade eight. Generally, among my grandfather's brothers and sisters, if they married someone who spoke English, their family was brought up English, if they married someone French, their family was brought up French. Wilfred married Bridget Hill, who immigrated on her own from Strabane, Ireland, in either 1914 or 1915. As a result, their family was brought up speaking English. They had three children, Ernest, Margaret, and Gerald. Gerald, known as Gerry, was the youngest, born on February 13, 1928.

Gerry, my father, lived for many years at 235 Rochester Street, a house his parents rented at the corner of Willow and Rochester. Only when my grandfather made a deal with his family to take care of his mother did my grandparents take over possession of 821 Gladstone Street in October 1933. This property had previously been willed to my great-grandfather, Alexander, and his brother Francis if they would agree to educate two younger brothers, George and James. So even though each generation acquired a major asset, there were heavy familial responsibilities associated with the transactions.

Later on, my grandmother saw a house she liked in the same area. My father remembers, "It was a really nice house, much better than the Gladstone house. She wanted to buy it. It cost less than one thousand dollars. Unfortunately, my father was always strongly influenced by the people he worked with at the Central Experimental Farm. The PhDs were like gods to him. He asked for their advice on the house. They told him not to buy it, because houses were going to go down in price! He told my grandmother, 'They know. They said we would be crazy to buy it now.'" And they never bought it. Once again, education does not necessarily equate with intelligence. My grandmother was a smart but uneducated woman. Too bad my grandfather did not listen to her.

In the early 1960s, my grandparents' home at 821 Gladstone Avenue was expropriated. According to my father, "Mayor Charlotte Whitton wanted to construct a new school for her alma mater, Commerce High School. Commerce had always been a poor cousin to Glebe High School. They built a new high school at the corner of Gladstone and Rochester. To enable this to happen, Whitton made a deal with St. Anthony's church to expropriate additional properties for a public housing development. My parents' property was part of the housing development expropriation. The quality of construction of the public housing was so poor that there are already plans to demolish and rebuild."

Some justified the expropriations as the demolition of slum housing to make way for newer housing. However, my father takes great exception to any suggestion that his parents' home was slum housing. "The area where they lived on Gladstone, east of Rochester, contained some of the best housing in the area. As you moved from Rochester to Preston on Gladstone, many of the houses were in poor shape and might be called a slum. This was an area with a lot of unemployment. So they tore down some good housing along with some poor housing. They also got rid of two churches, a Greek Orthodox Church and a Ukrainian Church." The only other church in the area, St. Anthony's Catholic Church, not only survived, but did very well for itself. My father believes that this is because the Italian community had a lot of political clout at that time. He says with some bitterness, "St. Anthony's endorsed the expropriation. They benefitted. They didn't lose a thing." He maintains that there were very few Italians in the area affected by the expropriation. "At that time, the Italian area was located between Balsam Street and Carling Avenue, near the Prescott Hotel. This was the area called Little Italy when I was young. So they never touched the main Italian area and they never touched the Italian church." Although my grandparents were devout Catholics, they did not attend St. Anthony's because it was there to serve the Italian community. My grandparents' parish was Our Lady of Perpetual Help on Eccles Street, across from St. Agatha's School. St. Agatha's, at the corner of Eccles and LeBreton, was the grade school my father attended.

The impact on the people expropriated was devastating. Clearly very upset, my father states, "This expropriation ruined my parents' old age! They had to move away from a close-knit community to a place where they didn't know anyone. In hindsight, we should have worked harder to find a new home close to the community." They had looked at a nice house and property near St. Mary's Church on Breezehill Avenue. It was located close to one of my grandfather's brothers, Alfie, who lived on Beech Street. My father says, "They had put in an offer and they thought they had the house. However, before the final paperwork was completed, someone else put in a higher offer. The seller came back to my father and asked him if he was willing to match the offer. My father said no. It was a big mistake, because it was really the place they wanted."

Once this deal fell through, my father's brother, Ernie, talked my grandparents into moving to Alta Vista. My uncle wanted them living near him. My father comments sadly, "They didn't know anyone there. They were unhappy. It was another big mistake." My grandfather did not live long after the move. He died of heart failure in 1966, just prior to his seventieth birthday. The day he died, my father recalls that he was talking to a colleague, Roy Taylor, in the office they shared. Roy took the phone call, then turned and said, "It's your mother and she wants to talk to you." She said, "Dad just died." My father rushed right over. When he arrived, his mother was there and his father was lying on the ground. The two of them had been working in the garden when my grandfather went around the corner of the house to turn the tap on for the garden hose. He didn't come back. When my grandmother looked around the corner, he was lying beside the tap. He died instantly. So, he died working in his garden. Interestingly, my father has told me several times that this would be his own ideal way to go. Both my paternal grandfather and great-grandfather died of massive heart attacks just before reaching the age of seventy. For many years, in the lead-up to my father's seventieth birthday, he was very worried about the same thing happening to him. It didn't matter how much we would remind him that his mother's family was very long lived, with many living well into their eighties and nineties. My grandmother was eighty-six when she died. She would have lived longer, but was so distraught over the early death of her only daughter that she gave up the will to live. It was a great relief to my father when he was able to celebrate that milestone birthday. After that, he never worried about it again.

✍ January 9, 1975 – heard today that Marg (his sister) has entered the hospital for an operation on an ovarian cyst.

✍ January 10, 1975 – Marg was operated on and had cancer. The doctor says she has 3 to 4 weeks at the most to live.

✍ January 14, 1975 – Marg died

🌣 March 2, 1975 – Mother seems very depressed since Marg's death.

🌣 August 8, 1975 – Mother's boarder phoned about 10 pm to say mother had a stroke. We went to the hospital. She seemed paralyzed and could not speak.

🌣 August 11, 1975 – About 9:30 am Marg (his wife) called and said to go straight to the hospital. Met Ernie, Trudy and priest there. About 10:15 am mother died.

🌣 December 31, 1975 – Bad year with Marg and mother dying.

My father comments, "When we were younger, my father was not much of a disciplinarian. He was a nice guy, but he completely opted out of making tough decisions. My mother raised the family. She was the money manager. My father would turn over his paycheque to her and she would look after everything. My father had a whole range of small entrepreneurial endeavours, such as selling Exhibition tickets, Christmas trees, and Christmas cards. The money he raised from these sources was what he used for beer and other things he wanted to do."

My father has come to realize, with the benefit of age and hindsight, how difficult his mother's circumstances were as a new immigrant to a strange country. "My mother's attitude was, she had a small amount of money to work with, and it was her job to manage it for a family of five. It couldn't have been easy." My grandmother had come from an even more impoverished situation in Ireland, but she still struggled to cope in Canada. From an early age, my grandmother would frequently say to my father and his sister, Margaret, "Just let Ernie have his way for peace and quiet." My father says, "If he didn't get what he wanted, Ernie made my mother's life miserable. He felt he was particularly deserving of things." My father is generally an easygoing person, so he was usually quite willing to go along with his mother's requests. "I was into sports and fishing. I came home for meals and then I was out the door again. My sister, Margaret, was the person my mother used to lean on and confide in." My father realizes now that he didn't provide much support to his mother. "She never confided in me. I was the youngest child. I wasn't interested in what my parents did. I never caused her any trouble, but I didn't do anything extra. I did the very minimum at home that I had to do."

I don't think my father was as lax as he would have us believe. He tells me that he worked at several jobs when he was quite young. All of his early earnings, he gave to his mother. His first job, at age nine, was as a delivery boy after school and during the summer at Hearn's Drug Store, located at the corner of Somerset and Booth. They would have orders for medication that needed delivery. "I could use my bicycle, since all the orders were within a short distance from the store. I would deliver the medication and collect the money. They would give me just enough money to make change when customers paid me." Until he was sixteen, he worked as a delivery boy or clerk for Somerset Grocery, followed by the Canadian National Telegraphs. At some point, he would have started to keep a certain part of the money he earned. All through university and until he got married, my father lived at home. During the school year, he lived in residence.

My father is not the same person he was when his mother asked him continually to defer to his brother's wishes. Looking back, he is sorry that he did not challenge his brother more. As he grew older, he did reach the stage where he would no longer let his brother manipulate him as he had growing up. In my uncle's mind, this change must have been caused by my mother's influence. This makes me laugh. Anyone that knows my mother at all would laugh too. She would not stand up to a fly. My father laments, "I don't think it was good for my brother that he was allowed to get his way all the time. It just enabled him and his behaviour became ingrained in him. It led him to believe it was an effective way to get what he wanted."

My father deeply regrets not taking much interest in how his parents felt and what they did. "I'm really sorry that I didn't do what you are doing with us with my mother and father. I'm particularly sorry that I never talked to my farther about the biggest thing in his life: his time serving during World War I. He enlisted in 1914, when he was seventeen or eighteen years old and served overseas in the army until 1918. He was in the trenches, subjected to gas attacks and mired in mud. But it was the highlight of his life. Before he went overseas, the furthest he had been away from home was Hog's Back and Black Rapids, which would have been in the far countryside of Ottawa in those days. After he returned, he never travelled again. My parents never even went away on a vacation in their entire life."

My father elaborates, "My father rarely talked about his war experience, but every November eleventh, he would put on his hat and his medals and go down to the War Memorial to participate in the ceremonies and march in the parade." He would have received a medal for volunteering, for serving overseas, and one each for serving in France and Germany. My mother remembers my grandfather once telling her, "I walked from France to Germany and back, and not once did I get a ride." As an indication of how much he valued this time in his life, my father recounts, "As soon as World War II was declared in 1939, without consulting my mother, or anyone else in the family, he tried to enlist again. They told him to go home and take care of his family."

About his mother, my father says, "I also know almost nothing about my mother's life in Ireland. I don't know why my mother emigrated, exactly when she came over, or how my parents met. When we were older, my brother and I offered to pay for a trip back to Ireland so that my mother could visit her family. She dismissed the offer, saying 'That's behind me. I don't ever want to go back there.' " My father believes that my grandmother had very bitter memories of her life there. Her children always felt she never wanted to talk about it. She kept in touch with some of her relatives, but it was infrequent. "My older sister, Margaret, may have known some of it," my father says. Unfortunately, when his sister died relatively young, at the age of forty-nine, any knowledge she had was also lost. My father laments, "I just never thought about it when they were alive." Since she was so reticent about talking about that time in her life, I ask my father if he thinks she might have talked about it if really pressed to do so. He pauses and thinks about it, then says, "Yes. I think that late in life she would have been more forthcoming." So many lost chances that I have chosen not to repeat.

2
EXPANDING HORIZONS

"I have always been interested in plants. It was my father's influence. He was the greenhouse man at the Central Experimental Farm. It was his whole life," my father says. So it could be said to be a natural progression from this early exposure that my own father would become a botanist.

Although he worked in the fields of the Central Experimental Farm as a summer job during high school, my father says that this did not influence his future plans. "It was purely a summer job. It was not something I looked forward to doing. We worked long hours during the summer, from 7 a.m. to 6 p.m., five days a week, and then on Saturday from 7 a.m. to 1 p.m., with no break for lunch." A favourite memory of his is how they would go straight from work to the Ottawa Rough Riders' football games, which started at 2 p.m. on Saturday afternoons.

It was my father's first job after senior matriculation (the equivalent of grade 13) that really started him in the direction of higher education. He worked for a company called Farley and Cassells. He worked for Mr. Sidney Farley, a civil engineer and land surveyor. Their office was located near the old Train Station on Rideau Street. Farley was the engineer for the Village of East View and Cassells was the engineer for the Village of Rockcliffe. There were several other more junior engineers on staff. My father comments, "Growing up, I didn't even know anyone that had gone to university and it had previously never entered my mind. This was my first exposure, for any length of time, to anyone who had gone to university." My father was Mr. Farley's gopher, doing all sorts of odd jobs, including acting as a chainman doing land surveys. "Although I was at the bottom of the ladder, I felt that what they were doing, I could learn to do," he says. His horizon began to expand with new possibilities. However, it was still hypothetical. After about eighteen months, it became obvious to my father that he was not going to go anywhere with Farley and Cassells.

This realization put my father in the right frame of mind to respond to a newspaper advertisement for jobs in the federal government. He decided to apply and wrote the general exam for entry into the public service. In 1947, at the age of nineteen, by chance he obtained a technician position working for a botanist, Dr. Clarence Frankton, at Agriculture Canada. Frankton was head of what was then called the Weed Investigations Unit at the Central Experimental Farm. When he started, my father wasn't earning any more than he had as a surveyor's assistant, but he quickly determined that he had more of a future working for Frankton.

Dr. Frankton was involved in taxonomy, the herbarium, and collecting plants. Assisting with these tasks became part of my father's job as a technician. Frankton liked collecting plants within the Ottawa district, but he did not enjoy going on collection trips further afield. As a result, my father did all the distant fieldwork. "In hindsight, this provided me with an opportunity I would not normally have had as a technician. Frankton always looked forward to when I returned from fieldtrips. As soon as I came in with the specimens, Frankton would rub his hands together and say, 'What did you get?' He just loved sorting through and discussing the plant material."

This was typical of my father; if there was a job to be done and my father thought he could do it, he would take it on. During the time he was a technician, two of the other botanists, Ray Moore and Wray Bowden ran into a big problem. They were both cytologists (studying the formation, structure, and function of cells). They had had a technician who was responsible for preparing material for their analysis. Unfortunately, this technician left suddenly and, of course, it takes a protracted time to go through the government bureaucratic process to get a replacement. "Ray Moore was a good friend of Clarie Frankton's," says my father. "One day, Frankton asked me if I would be willing to help him out. So, I started to learn how to prepare cytological material and ended up being quite good at it over an eight-month period." He had been doing the work for a while when Frankton called my father into his office to inform him, "I just wanted you to know that Bill Cody reported you to me. He said you were goofing off and running up to the third floor all the time. I told him he didn't know what he was talking about and to mind his own business because you were actually doing two jobs." It probably never entered Cody's mind that someone would be doing this. If he had known that my father would one day become his boss, he might have thought twice about trying to make trouble for him.

Soon after my father joined Agriculture Canada, he became friends with some of the other botanists. Two in particular, John Bassett and Doug Lindsay, he spent a lot of time with on various fieldtrips. His exposure to the work of these young scientists, along with the yearly crop of summer students, very soon stimulated my father's interest in going to university himself. In 1949, my father finally made the decision to quit his job in order to attend Macdonald College (part of McGill University). His choice of universities was influenced by where his mentor, Dr. Frankton, had received his PhD. My father comments, "This was a big decision for me. At that time, my contemporaries thought I already had a wonderful job. They couldn't believe I was quitting."

My grandfather's first response to hearing this news was to consult with some of the educated people he worked with at the Farm. What did they think about his son's desire to attend university? My father recounts, "They told my father that university was very difficult. One of the scientists had a son who had attended the Ontario Agricultural College at the University of Guelph and had failed." In my grandfather's mind, if the son of an educated person had failed, his own son would certainly not be able to do well at university. His advice to his son was that he would be wasting his time.

Fortunately, my grandmother was supportive of my father's plans. She counselled, "Don't listen to your father. Go ahead and give it a try." My grandmother had always lamented her own lack of a formal education. The educational trust that my grandmother set up for her deceased daughter's children, as part of her will, speaks volumes about her own lack of opportunities. I remember being extremely impressed with what she tried to do, even though it didn't work out as she would have hoped.

My father had also been quite active in extracurricular activities at the Farm. He was involved with both the volleyball and softball teams, as both a player and coach. He therefore had a wide circle of friends at the Farm who were supportive of his quest for a university education. They told him not to worry. They assured him that they would find a way to get him back as a summer student. His most important support came from his boss, Dr. Frankton. My father says, "He assured me that he would hold my technician position for me. This gave me the comfort of a fall-back position." If he was unsuccessful in his studies, my father knew he could return to his job. Frankton also agreed to sponsor him to return as a summer student. This gave my father a good sense of support as he stepped outside of his comfort zone. "In spite of all this, I was still very apprehensive about leaving my job," my father says. He became the first person in his family to attend university.

At that time, Macdonald College did not have a specialization in Botany. The nearest specialization was Plant Pathology. Therefore, when he graduated, my father did so as a plant pathologist, not a botanist. There were some courses in botany, but taking these ended up getting him into trouble. For about five years before and during the time he attended university, my father had worked under Dr. Frankton as both a technician and then as a summer student. In some areas of study, my father found that he knew more than the botany professor at Macdonald College did. This caused some embarrassing moments. In one of his classes on plant identification, the professor had labelled a selection of plant specimens. The problem was that many of them were actually misidentified. When my father tried to point this out, the professor did not appreciate his observations. "For the final exam, I actually had to memorize the wrong names for some of the plants in order to pass the course," he says with disgust.

My father started university in the second year of the program at Macdonald College because he had completed senior matriculation in Ontario, which included courses that were the equivalent of first year university in Quebec. The downside of this was that it had been three years since my father had finished high school and he had never even contemplated going back to school. "The information had all gone out of my mind," he says, "particularly certain subjects, like chemistry and physics, which required a lot of memory work." My father also did not get to benefit from refresher courses that he would have taken during the first year of the program. As a result, he found the first term very difficult. After Christmas, he felt more comfortable and even found time to play on the varsity hockey team, which meant frequent practices and away games. All this while forty percent of his classmates either failed or had to repeat second year. So all and all, he was relieved to find that he was settling into university life quite well.

Having a reliable summer job was critical to my father's ability to pay for his education. His family did not have the financial resources to assist him. So critical was the money to him that, with one exception, he literally started his summer job the day school finished and returned to school the day the term began. "The entire time I was at Macdonald College, I never took one day of holiday. I also took a payout for all the holidays I had accumulated based on the number of months I worked as both a technician and summer student. I was always very careful to leave work on a Monday, so that I would be paid for Saturday and Sunday too. The one exception was during my final year. I was playing varsity football and had to returned a little early for football practice." In spite of all this, my father was always on a tight budget, living hand-to-mouth. Because Macdonald College was not noted for the quality of its student meals, he says, "There were many, many times that I went to bed hungry."

My father reflects, "If someone at Farley and Cassells had been as supportive as Dr. Frankton, it is very likely that I may have become an engineer instead of a botanist." A perfect example of how the direction of your life can be influenced by the vagaries of the people you meet.

3
DEEP ROOTS AT THE FARM

The Mulligan family connections to the Central Experimental Farm in Ottawa are longstanding and broadly based. John Mulligan Senior and his wife, Elizabeth (nee Boyd), my great-great-great-grandparents, immigrated to Canada from County Down, Ireland, in 1842. They had nine children, three or four of whom were born in Ireland, with the rest born in Canada. All of the Mulligans in the Ottawa area are descendants of these nine children.

The original Mulligan farmstead was a thirty-four-and-a-half-acre piece of land on the Rideau River, south of Baseline Road. These lands were a "phantom lot" taken by the government for building the Rideau Canal, but missed during surveying and not officially recorded. John Mulligan Senior found out about this piece of land and laid claim to it by settling his family on it soon after they arrived in Canada. The property was officially purchased in 1860. Mulligan's Florist, on Prince of Wales Drive, is located on this piece of land, near the site of the original homestead.

A few years later, in 1868, John Senior purchased another thirty-five acres located north of Baseline Road, also fronting on the

Rideau Canal. The land had been canal reserve lands that were no longer required. A good portion of these lands would be expropriated in the formation of the Central Experimental Farm in 1886. The former Green Valley Restaurant was once located on part of the lands not expropriated. Green Valley Restaurant and Mulligan's Florist were both started and run by descendants of the brother who inherited the original Mulligan farm. When the Green Valley Restaurant burned down in the 2000s, it was still owned by a Mulligan (married name Stewart). Mulligan's Florist is still an active business but is no longer owned by a Mulligan family descendent. It was sold sometime in the last few decades. The new owner opted to maintain the original name.

My great-great-grandfather, John Mulligan Junior, was one of the children born in Ireland, in 1834, and was eight years old when the family immigrated to Canada. He was responsible for a branch of the Mulligan family becoming Roman Catholic. All of his siblings remained Protestant. The first census after John Senior arrived in Canada, showed him as Free Church, as in free from the influence of the pope. John Junior married Agnes Renaud who was born in Bytown in 1842.[1] Her parents, John Baptiste Renaud and Josephte St-Amour are listed in a French publication called *Bytown et ses pionniers canadiens-français* as one of the first French-Canadian families to reside in Bytown. They also had nine children, who curiously enough had the exact same names as John Junior's siblings, if in a different order. Agnes was Roman Catholic, and she brought up their children, including my great-grandfather, Alexander, in the Catholic faith with French as their first language.

John and Agnes, along with his brother George, settled on a farm on lot 20, Riverfront, Nepean Township, along the Rideau River, south of Black Rapids Creek. His brothers, Francis and Alexander, occupied the adjoining lands, lot 19. Both of these

---

[1] Until 1855, Ottawa was called Bytown.

properties were eventually expropriated by the National Capital Commission for the formation of the federal Greenbelt that wraps around the southern edge of Ottawa.

John Junior had a close relationship with his father, John Senior. Unfortunately, in 1888 at the age of fifty-four, John Junior was killed while working on his father's farm. He was in one of the barns during a thunderstorm. The barn was hit by a lightning strike. A large beam fell, killing him, making his wife a widow at a young age, with nine children to support. Agnes, a French-Canadian Catholic, was uncomfortable living among all the English-speaking Irish Protestants who made up her husband's family. Shortly before John Junior died, the couple had bought a ten-acre parcel of land in a subdivision of lot K, called Nepeanville, on the site of the present Arboretum. A developer was planning a subdivision primarily for French labourers who had worked on the building of the Rideau Canal. However, the land was expropriated as part of the formation of the Central Experimental Farm in 1886. Agnes then bought property in Rochesterville, where many of her family lived. She lived on Pine Avenue, which is now Gladstone Avenue, until her death in 1894. The streets were named after different trees because of its status as a lumber area. The family continued to live in this area for several generations. My father remembers his grandmother and several of his uncles also owning property on Pine Street or the next street over, Balsam Avenue.

Living in such close proximity to the Central Experimental Farm, several generations of the Mulligan family have worked there, not surprisingly. My great-grandfather, Alex, was farm foreman of all the field staff. My father recalls, "He was in charge of what they called the 'bull gang'. If there was a job on the farm that had to be done, the bull gang did it. They did the dirty jobs. They are the ones that painted all the fence posts red with white caps." My grandfather, Wilfred, and several of his brothers also worked there. My father's uncle, Alphie, was in charge of the main cattle barn. Another uncle, Clifford, the youngest of the brothers, had scarlet fever when he was young. As a result, he had a low IQ, but was happy to work on various labouring jobs at the Farm. My father thinks that other family members may have worked at the Farm at various times, possibly even his uncle Nelson, who later moved to the United States. With virtually no education, he ended up becoming a multi-millionaire. Uncle Nelson owned, at one time, the largest Ford dealership in the world, in Dearborn, Michigan. Or his uncle Walter, who was a champion speed skater. He also moved to the United States to work for Nelson.

My grandfather was responsible for the Cereal Greenhouse at the Central Experimental Farm, next to the Ornamental Gardens. He took this job very seriously. My father remembers, "I had a very close relationship with my father. When I was two or three years old, he would take me places on the handlebars of his bicycle. On Saturday and Sunday, we would go to the Farm to water the plants in the greenhouse. I would wander around the greenhouse while my father worked." My father also remembers his father taking him out to the field south of the Booth Barn, between Prince of Wales Drive and the Rideau Canal. The field extended right down to the Canal. The Cereal Division used to grow grain species there during the summer. "The most precious material, new varieties that they were trying to multiply, were grown in a big cage, about fifteen by thirty feet in size and eight feet tall. The cage was made of wire mesh, with openings small enough to make it difficult for birds to enter the cage, but open enough to allow sufficient sunlight to reach the plants. In spite of this, birds would still sometimes get into this cage. It was my father's job to get them out. He had a shotgun that he used to get rid of crows in the cereal fields. They kept the gun in a big locked box in the building next to the cereal greenhouse. I remember my father unlocking the box and taking out the gun. You have to remember, at that time, in the 1930s, the Farm was located outside the limits of the City of Ottawa. Once you were south of Carling Avenue, you were in the countryside."

The Cereal Division would also ship some of the seed, from the important new varieties they were trying to multiply, down to Mexico on a regular basis. This was to speed up multiplication of the seed by growing plants during the Canadian winter. My father says, "I remember there being some talk about my father going down to Mexico, but he never did or wanted to go. He was not the adventuresome type. Now they have more sophisticated ways of multiplying varieties."

My father has worked at the Farm in many capacities for seven decades and counting. Early on, he worked in the fields as a summer student while he was in high school. He thinks that his grandfather, Alex, may have still been working at the Farm at that time. After he finished high school, he worked for a short period in 1945 and 1946 as a technician, followed by a couple of years as a summer student while he attended university, before finally returning as a biologist, research scientist, and eventually Director of the Biosystematics Research Institute.

I am the only member of succeeding generations that continued any involvement with the Farm. In 1975, I worked for the summer in the Agriculture Canada library at the Sir John Carling Building. Ten years later, in 1985, the consulting firm I was working for won the competition to design the centennial chrysanthemum show. I was the landscape architect for this project. As always, my parents were very supportive.

- Aug. 9, 1985 – Julie phoned about 6:30 pm to tell us that her company was awarded the contract for the 1986 Mum Show.

- Oct. 16, 1986 – I dropped around and saw the start of Julie's centennial mum show. I and the others are quite impressed.

- Oct. 29, 1986 – I went to the opening of the mum show. Everyone agreed that Julie's design was terrific.

I was curious to know if my father's decision to take the Government of Canada employment test, which led to his

19

working at the Central Experimental Farm, was influenced by the family tradition of working there. He laughs and says, "No, it was just an opportunity. I could have ended up anywhere after passing the exam. I never even thought about the tradition aspect." That said, he certainly felt comfortable working at the Farm because he had spent so much time there with his father.

There was some overlap in the time that my father and grandfather worked at the Farm. My mother recalls my grandfather still working there when they were first married. When I ask what my grandfather thought of his son working there as a scientist, my father says that he never articulated anything about this, and my father never thought to ask him. On reflection, my father believes that his father never came to think of his son as smart, despite his success at university. Two of his uncles, Alfie and Clifford, were also still working there. In fact, Clifford was still working there when my father retired in 1987. He did odd jobs around the farm. He was well liked and earned the nickname of Big Clifford. Although they were all working at the Farm at the same time for a while, my father says that they never interacted. They worked in completely different realms. My father comments, "When you think that when I retired I was Acting Director General of all the institutes, including the Animal Research Farm in the Greenbelt, it would have been inconceivable to my father, that's for sure!"

Even in my lifetime, I am aware that there was a time when the Central Experimental Farm was a more dynamic, much loved place to work. There was a real sense of community among the people working at the Farm. It was a much more social place. There were many Farm sports teams and I fondly remember a huge family picnic held in the lower Arboretum each summer. I ask my father if he knows when and why this began to change. "The change was gradual," he says. "The old guard absolutely revered the Farm. A similar sentiment is absent now." My father further contemplates the question and then comes up with at least four major reasons for this change.

First, he feels that most of the recent senior managers have no interest at all in the Central Experimental Farm. "It used to be that the farming industry had a lot of political clout. Most of the early managers came from western Canada's wheat and farming country. They cared about agriculture, so the experimental farm system was important to them. For most of the current managers, it is just a job." This also applies to the rank and file staff working at the Farm. "A lot of the labourers in the early days, worked there part-time," he says. "They were farm people from the Ottawa area who worked at the Farm to supplement their income. They would come to plant or harvest the crops. So, it has gone from being a place that was primarily farm oriented, with people that loved farming, to people primarily interested in career advancement. The current philosophy that prevails is that you don't have to know about farming or research, you just have to know how to manage." My father just shakes his head at this wrong-headed notion.

Second, my father says that when he was young, from the 1930s to 1960s, the number of people working at the Farm was much smaller. Everyone knew each other. If you were a social person, like my father, it was easy to know people all over the Farm. He was involved in many sports. As the Farm grew and became more complex, the sense of community diminished. At one time, virtually all the research at the Farm was located in the Saunders Building. The Director General of the entire Central Experimental Farm also had his office in that building.

The third reason is that there used to be a lot fewer rules to follow. "Things happened then, that nowadays would be considered high risk. For example, the Farm used to raise turkeys, chickens, and geese for experimental purposes. When they were finished with the birds, they would give them to staff at Christmas to take home. Now, we are a lot more aware of health and safety issues associated with doing this type of thing. The Farm also had a dairy, where milk produced from their dairy herd, was processed. It was located across from the main barns, which is now the Agricultural Museum." My father remembers when he was a summer student during high school, the fieldworkers used to bring their lunch, but go to the dairy to buy their milk. They could buy a pint of pasteurized milk for almost nothing. My father even worked in the dairy for a short period one summer. One of the regular staff was on holidays and they needed someone to pitch in.

Finally, in my father's opinion, the single biggest factor that changed the Farm was the 1967 move of the National Headquarters of the Department of Agriculture from downtown Ottawa to the Sir John Carling Building at the Central Experimental Farm. This meant that all the administrative staff and the Minister of Agriculture, who had previously been located in the Confederation Building at the corner of Wellington and Bank, were all now located on the Farm. "Prior to their arrival, the Farm had run itself. Suddenly, all these administrators started to get very involved in the day-to-day operation of the Farm. These people didn't know much about the Farm and had other priorities. This changed the whole character of the Farm," he says.

The Sir John Carling Building is the newest building at the Farm, completed in 1967. It could be a case of bad karma, but due to a variety of deficiencies, including asbestos insulation, poor air quality, and poor temperature control, it was vacated in 2007. More than ten years ago, in anticipation of the closure of the Sir John Carling Building, some of the staff were moved to the Saunders Building. In describing the move, my father recounts, "They displaced some of the botanists and almost all of the mycologists to the Neatby Building and took over one wing of the second floor of the Saunders Building. In doing so, they installed steel doors with combination locks to secure access to their area of the building and spent millions of dollars renovating the space." My father goes on to say, "They weren't there more than six months when management decided the administration staff were too far away and moved them back temporarily to the Sir John Carling Building. With the second floor empty, they decided to move other staff from the Sir John Carling Building there. So they renovated it all over again. They moved in, and now they are gone again. The second floor is empty again." My father just shakes his head at the ridiculousness of the situation. The only reason they weren't able to move all of the botanists and mycologist out of the Saunders Building is because the National herbarium is there. The Saunders Building is an old records building and, as a result, the floors were reinforced to support the big steel cases.

One of the things my father laments is the decline of horticulture at the Farm. When he started as a technician at Agriculture Canada in 1947, horticulture was one of the main divisions, along with botany, plant pathology, chemistry, and cereal and field husbandry. Horticulture is the science and technology of cultivating ornamental plants. At the Farm, this included the selection of species from other countries and the breeding of new hybrids and cultivars well suited to the cold Canadian climate. Selections ranged from those best suited for farm shelterbelts, hedges, fruit and shade trees, flowering shrubs, and perennials. In addition to carrying out horticultural research, the horticultural division was also responsible for the annual Chrysanthemum Show.

The real decline in horticulture began in the late 1980s. My father says with regret, "This was a period of severe budgetary reduction. Those in charge at the time had to make decisions on where to make cuts. To many of these managers, horticulture was not considered to be really agriculture." Eventually, many of the horticultural programs at the Central Experimental Farm were transferred to various other research stations across Canada. One of the last programs to fade out was the Chrysanthemum Show. The reason it was kept for so long, well after many other horticultural programs, was that it was a well-loved annual tradition. My father confirms, "They resisted getting rid of it for many years due to public demand for it."

Now things are coming full circle. A 2009 Deloitte & Touche report on the impact of ornamental horticulture on Canada's economy found that only Alberta and Saskatchewan have a higher Gross Domestic Product contribution from what is considered real agriculture, crop production, than from ornamental horticulture production. Horticulture and horticulture-related tourism are rising in importance, fed by an aging population with lots of money and leisure time. A new national botanic garden is actively being planned on a thirty-four-acre site at the Central Experimental Farm. While the Farm may never reach the pinnacle of importance that it once held in the field of Canadian horticultural research, it may yet evolve again into a dynamic centre of horticultural excellence.

4
THE COLLEGE EXPERIENCE

In 1949, my father entered the agricultural program at Macdonald College, a campus of McGill University located in Ste.-Anne-de-Bellevue, Quebec. In addition to expanding his intellectual horizons, Macdonald College was a great social experience for my father, and most noteworthy as the place he met my mother.

My mother, Margaret (nee McDonald) started at Macdonald College one year ahead of my father because she had attended high school in Quebec. They ended up in the same year, he in Agriculture, and she in Dietetics. Although they were in different programs, they had some of the same classes. While my father certainly knew her as a classmate, during his first two years at Macdonald he was dating another woman, Anna Brown, also in Agriculture but a year ahead. She graduated before my father and he lost track of her. In his final year, he asked my mother out. My mother says that she remembers seeing Anna and my father together. She thought they were serious. Many years later, when my father was Director of the Biosystematics Research Institute, one of the botanists, Dr. Susan Aiken, returned from a fieldtrip in western Canada. She gleefully announced that she had met his old girlfriend, a naturalist in Prince George, British Columbia. It turned out that my father once identified a *draba* specimen that Anna had sent to the Institute. Her surname had changed, so he hadn't made the connection.

My mother had never intended to go to Macdonald College but rather the main campus of McGill University, in Montreal, for a Bachelor of Arts. She had good marks, but failed French in her final year. She didn't find out until well into August. "I wasn't suddenly going to be good in French," she says. At that time, French was an essential requirement to attend McGill. She agonized over what to do. To compound the problem, in that era, Catholics couldn't attend many universities, and the options for women were even fewer. Finally, her father suggested, "You could go to Macdonald College. They don't require French." He was aware of this because his two youngest brothers, Duncan and Alex, were both graduates of Macdonald College in Agriculture, Duncan in 1939 and Alex in 1942. They both later proceeded on to postgraduate studies elsewhere. So she followed her father's advice, and never regretted the decision, illustrating how little quirks in the system can influence the course of a person's life.

When my parents attended Macdonald College, it was not only a very Anglophone institution, but a very Protestant one as well. As two of the very few Catholic students attending the college, they were a minority. My father says that he never felt like a minority, but that my mother probably did. When my mother started in home economics at Macdonald College, she was interviewed and told that there were two streams in the program: teaching home economics or hospital dietetics. However, when they found out that she was Catholic, she was unequivocally told, "Oh, you can't go into teaching, you're Catholic. You have to go into the hospital program." This was because all the teaching positions were in Protestant schools.

When I ask my father if he attended church while he was at

college, his immediate response is "Oh yes. At that point in my life, I was very religious. Later, I became more and more disillusioned." He remembers his roommate, Paul Aird, making a few sly remarks about his Catholic faith. My father comments, "It seemed to amuse him that I went to church every Sunday." My mother says that my father once told her that church is where he first noticed her. My father in turn confirms this.

My father's first meeting with his future in-laws was courtesy of an invitation to Sunday lunch. When this invitation was extended, he was not only going to decline but was seriously considering ending their relationship. This rift occurred because of the college's annual Sadie Hawkins Day dance. My father was a candidate for King Abner that year, so he was required to attend the event. They had been dating for long enough that he certainly expected his girlfriend to ask him to the dance. "But she didn't. Someone else asked me to go with her, and I accepted. What was I supposed to do? I thought she's not interested enough to ask me, so I'll go with someone else." Apparently, my mother did end up asking him, but at the last minute. Anyone who knows my father knows that he is not one to wait to do anything until the last minute. He told her, "No, I have already said that I am going with someone else."

My father was voted King Abner. This event was well documented in the annual college yearbook. The page with a photo of Dad as King Abner was well thumbed by my brothers and me. It was a source of both amusement and horror to see our father kissing a woman who was not our mother. I don't think my mother was particularly upset about not going to the dance. She is a timid person and has always been uncomfortable in social situations with large numbers of people. Instead of being upset that her boyfriend was going to the dance with another girl, she asked him, "I'm planning on going home this weekend. Would you come for Sunday lunch?" At that point, my father was not in a good frame of mind about the future of their relationship. "I did go," he says, "because she asked me. I wasn't happy about the situation, but I took the train into Montreal."

At that time, my mother's parents lived in Westmount, an upscale neighbourhood in Montreal. Her father was an electrical engineer with Bell Telephone. This relative affluence was quite a contrast to my father's humble background. When I enquire if he was intimidated, his response is a definite "No, I am not that easily intimidated." My mother heartily agrees, "He could not care less about things like that." When I asked my father what swung the relationship back onto a good course, his immediate response is "Mrs. McDonald's good meals!" My mother agrees. "My mother was the best cook I ever knew. Some people can produce good meals occasionally, but she produced good meals every day."

During the entire time my father was in university, he never thought about getting married. He certainly dated women who weren't Catholic. "I was a very social guy," he says. "I got around and knew a lot of people." My mother concurs, "He never professed that I was his first girlfriend." When my mother asserts that he was her first boyfriend, my father immediately refutes this. She finally admits, "I dated a bit, but not much." Asked when he knew his relationship with my mother was serious, my father says, "Slowly." They started dating during their last year of university, 1951, but didn't get married until 1954.

When my parents attended Macdonald College, the only student housing was on-campus residences. My father's roommate for the entire time was Paul Aird. The two had a common bond in that they both started in the second year of the program. Aird, whose home was in Hudson, Quebec, had spent two years at the University of New Brunswick in Forestry before transferring to Macdonald College to study soil conservation. My father had completed senior matriculation in Ontario, which qualified him to enter the second year of university in Quebec.

He and Aird got along well from the start. They had many of the same interests. For his part, Aird says, "I was pleased to have him as a roommate because he was so easy to get along with. Gerry was very popular with everyone." My father says, "Paul was a loner, while I was more inclined to be part of the gang. He was certainly accepted by the various crowds because he was confident enough of himself. He wasn't isolated by any means. He chose to do things alone."

Aird was also a renowned jokester. My father recounts, "He would do devious things and he wouldn't tell anyone about them. I would find out afterwards, sometimes quite a bit afterwards and only because we were roommates. He used to set the fire alarm off in the men's residence. He did this a couple of times by sticking a pin between two wires, which triggered the alarm. He told me about doing this, but probably no one else ever knew." My mother was a recipient of one of his pranks, "Paul Aird dumped my bed in residence in our fourth year." Aird is quick to confirm his reputation as a major prankster, "Oh yes, I was!" He has his own favourite memories. "We released greased pigs in the women's residence." He maintains he was just a helper, and that it was someone else who had all the ideas. "There was a little group that I worked with. We never told anyone about what we did."

Smoking was another thing the roommates had in common in those days. For my father, smoking is a distant memory. "When I was young, a lot of people smoked. It was very common. I think I was in my teens when I first started." When my father stops to think about it now, he realizes how crazy it was, especially when he was at Macdonald College. "The meals at the college were terrible. I was starving a lot of the time, and instead of spending what little money I had on food, I would end up buying cigarettes." Both he and Aird were chronically very short of funds. Aird says, "We often borrowed smokes from each other." Aird had a sister and brother who would occasionally send him five or six dollars. "When they did, it was like winning the lottery," he says.

About twenty years later, in 1968, when my father became aware of all the health effects of smoking, he thought, "I'm not going to live long if I keep doing this. So, I just decided to stop." And in typical style, once he made the decision, it only took him two weeks to quit. He was incensed when no one in the family noticed. He has never been able to relate to people who require all kinds of aids to help them stop. I think that he severely underestimates his high level of self-discipline, a quality that many others do not have.

Over the years, the two roommates have managed to maintain a life-long friendship, staying in touch through regular Christmas cards, irregular phone calls and visits, and frequent Macdonald College reunions.

Paul Aird also tells me, "Gerry was a very good hockey player. I was proud of my roommate for his ability to play varsity hockey and football, as well as other sports." In those days, sports were a big part of university life for everyone at Macdonald College. My mother was one of the exceptions. Growing up, my mother did not participate in sports. She attributes this to having attended only Catholic schools. Unlike public schools, in those days Catholic schools rarely had gyms. She found that most of her college classmates had a lot of experience playing on teams. My father says that this lack of a gymnasium is why he never played much basketball, an indoor sport. Hockey, baseball, and football were all outdoor sports that didn't require a gym, so those are the sports he played.

Until she met my father, my mother had been too timid to try any of the many sports played at Macdonald College. After they had dated for a while, my father encouraged her to join the women's intramural hockey team, which he coached. She says, "It was fun. I liked it. I would never have tried it if it wasn't for your father." Dad proudly reports, "She was my second best player! She played forward. We actually had a pretty good team.

She went on to join the track team and was also a good runner."

Until the Ottawa Senators were formed, with the exception of one rebel brother, my entire family had always been avid Montreal Canadiens fans. The Toronto Maple Leafs were, and still are, personae non gratae in our family. My brother Don states, "We were big Montreal Canadiens fans, for years and years and years. I remember all the names — Lafleur, Lapointe, and Cournoyer, and the numbers and all the Stanley Cups they won. As much as there was loving the Habs, there was hating the Leafs."

I was very shocked then to hear that my paternal grandfather was a life-long Leafs fan. How could this be! It happened because when my grandfather was growing up, Foster Hewitt broadcast the Toronto Maple Leafs games every Saturday night on English radio. At that time, this was all that was available. This was a bit surprising given that my grandfather was raised in a French-speaking family. Even more shockingly, my own father admits to being a Leafs fan when he was young because of listening to these games with his father. This changed for my father when he attended Macdonald College, but my grandfather remained a staunch Leafs fan until the day he died.

At Macdonald College, one of the men on the varsity hockey team, Paul Dopp, had played for St. Michaels, a junior farm team for the Toronto Maple Leafs. Several of his teammates, including Red Kelly, went on to play in the National Hockey League. He ended up with friends on several teams in the league. When these friends played in Montreal, they supplied Dopp with tickets. As a friend, my father was often asked to attend games with him. My Dad would never have been able to afford a ticket with his own limited funds. These were the days when Rocket Richard was at the pinnacle of his career. Quite a few of the other students at the college were from Montreal and thus avid Montreal Canadiens fans. The more he attended their games, the more my father grew to become a fan and the more he disliked the Leafs. So, in other words, all became right in the world. This wonderful opportunity did not last long. My father laments, "Paul Dopp, along with quite a few other players on the varsity hockey team failed their year. This was also the end of a really terrific varsity hockey team." This brief friendship did however lead to a lifetime divergence in his national hockey team allegiance.

Growing up, I only ever heard great stories from both my parents about their time at Macdonald College. I always felt that they had had the time of their lives there. They both concur. My mother is quick to comment, "I loved it. It was a small campus." My father agrees, "Yes, I had a good time. I enjoyed it." My mother then pipes up with, "I didn't enjoy it as much as he and Paul Aird did!" Paul Aird concurs, "They were good years, memorable years."

5
BECOMING A RESEARCH SCIENTIST

The scientific community is often distinguished by its excessive and misplaced obsession with academic credentials. While this presents a major and often unsurpassable obstacle for many a graduate with a lowly Bachelor of Science, for my father it was just one more challenge to tackle.

In 1952, my father graduated from Macdonald College with a Bachelor of Science. This qualified him as a biologist. Then, as now, becoming a research scientist requires a PhD. My father had already been a mature student in university. Soon after graduation, he married and my parents immediately started a family. He did not feel able to return to university then and he never did, even though he had opportunities to do so as time went on.

From the beginning, my father observed that a certain number of scientists with PhDs virtually stopped learning the day they graduated. This was particularly evident to him later on, during his time as Director of the Biosystematics Research Institute. "University only provides you with the foundation. Upon graduation you are only getting started. There is a lot to learn and you should take advantage of learning as much as you can, any way you can, and never stop learning," he says. This was often his advice to new staff. He has seen many people arrive with a PhD figuring that they had made it and didn't have to put in any further effort. "They don't keep up with the latest research. They don't advance themselves. Everything passes them by. You see about twenty-five percent of new graduates improve, while ten years later the other seventy-five percent are still doing the same old thing they were doing when they left university," he asserts.

My father, on the other hand, decided early on that he would always strive to learn. Therefore, in his quest to become a research scientist, he gathered all the research papers of the top botanists in the world in his field of study: Edgar Anderson, G. Ledyard Stebbins, J.D. Clausen, David Keck, and William Hiesey.

Edgar Anderson (1897–1969), was an American botanist who wrote *Introgressive Hybridization* in 1949, an original and important contribution to botanical genetics. His research focused on developing techniques to quantify geographic variations of species. Anderson did a lot of work on how various new entities were formed by hybridization between species and how genes would be incorporated.

G. Ledyard Stebbins (1906–2000), was an American botanist and geneticist, regarded as one of the leading evolutionary biologists of the twentieth century. Stebbins did a lot on the classification of plants, as well as the evolution of various species and families.

A group of three scientists working in California, J.D. Clausen, David Keck, and William Hiesey, conducted scientific transplant studies to show that plants of the same species collected from different locations behave quite differently. They published their work in a 1940 groundbreaking paper called "Experimental studies on the nature of species: I. Effects of varied environments on Western North American plants."

34

Before their work, people had thought that a particular species was the same no matter where it grew. If you have a plant with a distribution from Canada to Mexico, chances are that if you took representative plants of that species from various locations and subjected them to the same growing conditions in Ottawa, some plants would be winter hardy and some would die. This difference among populations of the same species is common knowledge today, but was a revolutionary idea in 1940.

My father avidly read the work of these scientists to discover what they were doing and what techniques they were using. One-by-one, he tried using the same techniques. He also came to understand the importance of research scientists reviewing the literature to see how their results stack up to that of other researchers. "If they don't do this, it is not proper science," he says.

In spite of all this, as a biologist, my father was not expected, nor entitled, to write research papers, but because he had a lot of knowledge, he started to write and publish research papers anyway. After a few years, he was starting to publish more papers, in more prestigious research journals, than most of his botanical colleagues. The turning point in his career came when he gave a paper at the *1st Symposium on General Biology* organized by the International Union of Biological Sciences held at Asilomar, California, in 1964. Most of the other participants were giants in genetics, at that time, including many of those whose research he was following. My father revelled in being among them, talking to them. "It was a heady experience for me. When I first arrived, I was a little apprehensive, but felt that I had something to offer in my field," he says. He had submitted a paper on what he had been working on, and it was accepted. He was the only Canadian invited to participate. Papers given at the symposium titled *The Genetics of Colonizing Species* were later published in book form in 1965. His reputation in Agriculture Canada and elsewhere took off after that. The experience had a huge impact on his professional confidence.

Not only was my father the only Canadian invited, he was also one of the youngest contributors to the resulting book. Because of this, he thinks that he may very well be one of the few contributors still alive. "Certainly, those I knew well have all died," he says. The book is still considered an important textbook in plant genetics. Evidently this is correct. In May 2014, I stumbled upon a notice that the *Molecular Ecology Journal* had organized a conference to celebrate "the 50th anniversary of one of the most important books in evolutionary biology: *The Genetics of Colonizing Species* (1965) edited by Herbert Baker and G. Ledyard Stebbins. This classic volume was based on a symposium at Asilomar, California in 1964 and initiated the study of the genetics and evolution of invasive species. To revisit the historical legacy of the meeting and book, we are pleased to announce a symposium at Asilomar from August 13-15, 2014." My father was very interested and pleased to hear this news.

Outside of the Research Institute, everyone else in the world reading my father's research papers assumed he had a PhD; he even started to receive letters addressed to Dr. Mulligan. The symposium also led to many outside opportunities, such as an invitation to chair a session at an international conference. Further invitations snowballed from there. These included invitations to contribute his expertise to a wide range of biological and botanical organizations. Over time, a shortlist of these included roles as Treasurer, Director, Vice-President, and President of the Canadian Botanical Association, a member of the Editorial Board of *Davidsonia*, and compiler for The International List of Plant Chromosome Numbers. He became sought after and, as a result, he gained more and more confidence. While initially not receiving the same recognition in Canada, my father decided to continue his research whether he was rewarded for it or not. Eventually, he had so many papers and had been so active in his field that he was reclassified from Biologist to Research Scientist.

Another major factor in my father achieving this reclassification was his early request for a copy of the job specifications for a Research Scientist. Once he received this information, he made a point of systematically doing all of the things that a research scientist was required to do. A research scientist is someone who publishes reputable research papers, someone who takes an active role in scientific societies and becomes an executive in those societies. What my father did was try to make his case for fulfilling all of the job requirements for the position stronger than anybody else for that classification. Then he insisted that he be put forward for reclassification to the Inter-departmental Committee. Even though some people said, "You don't have a PhD and therefore you don't qualify," he insisted on going forward to test to see if he could do it.

The Inter-departmental Committee is a national committee with representation from across Canada. The committee is part of the annual review process where research scientists are evaluated for various promotions as they move through four potential classification levels. Not every scientist was put forward for evaluation, only those who were recommended by their Institute or Station Director. The Committee would review and evaluate each submission. Just because someone was recommended did not mean that he or she would be promoted. For certain levels, such as for Research Scientist 4, there was a quota. Only five percent of the research scientists in Canada were allowed to become RS4 at any one time. In fact, when you arrived at the committee meeting each year, the first thing you would find out was how many openings for RS4 there would be available that year. My father says, "If you didn't have a PhD it was almost impossible to become a Research Scientist 4." The fact that he eventually did so is just one more testament to his abilities and tenancy.

✍ March 5, 1976 – received formal notification of my promotion to RS4. I have now reached the highest level for a researcher in the Federal Government, a goal that I never thought possible in my wildest imagination.

The Inter-departmental Committee makes these decisions based on the submitted information in front of them. My father used this technique to move through four levels of classification and at the highest classification, Senior Research Scientist, actually earned more than the Director position he eventually occupied. This approach required my father to prepare such good documentation that it would make it difficult for formal recognition of his achievements to be denied. "I was willing to take the chance and was not worried about being embarrassed," he states.

According to Stephen Darbyshire, a biologist still working in the Institute, one of the main bones of contention of my father's detractors was his lack of a PhD. Darbyshire says that one of the things he will always remember is a comment made by Dr. John McNeill, a former Section Head with Agriculture Canada. McNeill was commenting on scientists at the Central Experimental Farm who did not have a PhD. "Although he did not mention any names, it was clear who he was speaking about. He said something to the effect that among the non-PhD scientists, some have earned a PhD many times over." Darbyshire considers this high praise for my father's abilities as a scientist.

Dan Brunton, a well-known consulting field naturalist in the Ottawa area, cites other scientists, such as Cliff Crompton and Don Lafontaine, as having followed similar career paths to my father at the Central Experimental Farm. According to Brunton, my father played a big role in Lafontaine becoming an internationally renowned research scientist. Brunton thinks it is no coincidence that both my father and Crompton were always very encouraging of untraditional research and researchers. "They were far more open to helping people walking in off the street than the traditional PhD researcher," Brunton states. This assistance was critical to him during the early years of his development as a naturalist. Brunton greatly appreciates their assistance.

Rosanna (Menchini) Carson, my father's executive secretary during the time he was Director, recalls that some of the scientists resented that my father didn't have a PhD, yet he was able to become Director. My father says, "I always wondered about that. I didn't feel people were so much resentful as embarrassed at times. For instance, when we used to meet with scientists at the Smithsonian Institute in Washington, everyone else in the group had a PhD except me. I think it was embarrassing for them that the head of their group didn't have one. I never took it personally. The reality was, at the time, there wasn't a scientist with a PhD who had the management capabilities I had. All the Smithsonian staff called me Dr. Mulligan. They just assumed that I had a PhD. Everyone I corresponded with from around the world also addressed me as Dr. Mulligan. I never presented myself as such, they just assumed it. Even those who knew I wasn't a doctor, called me that anyways, because they were more comfortable doing so. It was their hang up, not mine, so I just went along with it."

With so many fixated on reaching the pinnacle of academic achievement, it is interesting to discover that not everyone wanted to become a research scientist.

✍ September 25, 1981 – Allyson does not want to go back for her PhD.

Such a person was Suzanne Allyson. Allyson had a bachelor's degree in entomology and worked as a biologist in the *lepidoptera* (butterflies and moths) section. The previous director, Dr. John Hardwick, had wanted her to go back to university for her PhD. Agriculture Canada was even willing to sponsor her to do so. However, she kept putting it off and putting it off. Hardwick kept pushing her to do it. Finally, when my father took over as Director, he asked her, "Do you really want to go back and get a PhD to become an entomologist and do taxonomy?" She was quick to reply, "No! I'm having a nervous breakdown over this." My father then asked, "Are you content to be a biologist?" Her immediate response was "Yes! I don't want to go back to school." My father replied, "Fine. I will put you in charge of the identification service." She eventually left Agriculture Canada to take another job. Years later, Allyson sent my father a nice note telling him that he had turned her whole life around.

> ⚕ April 26, 1995 – I talked to Pat Mavis and she told me that Suzanne Allyson, her neighbour, said that, as Director, I changed her whole life for the better.

One of the things that helped my father reach his goals was his willingness to try anything. "If an opportunity came up, even if I wasn't too sure if I was able to do it, I found it much easier to try than to say no. I would hate to say there was something I wanted to do and didn't because I wasn't sure if I was able to do it, or might find it difficult. Failure never bothered me, but having regrets did. It is something I have done all of my life," he says. My father cites this, probably more than any other trait, as responsible for any successes he has had. This is an understanding of himself that he only gained as he grew older and looked back on his life. This drive to try things evolved, at least partially, in response to his observations of his own father. He comments, "I always felt that my father never realized his potential. Anything he did, he did very well. However, he was not a person who could stand failure. He was fearful of trying new things." My father was never sure if this was really a fear of failure or just a lack of ambition. In either case, it left a lasting impression on him.

In my opinion, the quality that most defines my father's approach to many things in his life, including his quest to become a research scientist, is his persistence. He just doesn't give up easily. "When I get disappointed," he says, "I am down for a little while, but it doesn't take much of a spark to get me going again. Then I'm ready to start over again, full of vim, vigour, and vitality. Most people aren't like this. If they experience a setback, they give up. I don't."

6
THE RESEARCH SCIENTIST

In 2006, Gerald Alfred Mulligan won the *George Lawson Medal*. First awarded in 1969, this medal is the most prestigious award of the Canadian Botanical Association. Its stated goal is, "...to provide a collective, formal expression of the admiration and respect of botanists in Canada for excellence in the contribution of an individual to Canadian botany."

There are three areas in botany in which my father is considered an expert. People outside of Ottawa typically only know him for one of these areas of expertise, usually because they work in that specific field. First, he is recognized as one of the foremost authorities on *Brassicaceae* for Canada, including weedy, wild, and cultivated mustards. Second, he has almost certainly determined the chromosome number of more different species of plants in North America than any other botanist. Finally, he has worked extensively on the biology of weeds.

Many people know my father for his work on the classification and biology of mustard (*Brassicaceae*). He is the Canadian mustard expert. When someone is considered an authority on a plant, he or she is a specialist on that plant or family of plants. Plant authorities typically have published many research papers on the plant and may have described new species in the family. They would have accumulated a considerable body of work. This expertise is usually regional; it is seldom worldwide.

Brassicaceae is a family that, in general terms, has pods, four flower petals, and six stamens of which four are long and two are short. There are also species of mustard that only have four stamens. Currently, the family is called *Brassicaceae*, but when my father first became a botanist, it was known as *Cruciferi*, based on the crucifix. Gradually they changed the name because the people in charge of nomenclature in plants decided rightly or wrongly that the family should have as the type genus the same name as the family. The type genus for the mustard family is *Brassica*, so it was called *Brassicaceae*.

In Canada and the Northern United States my father eventually became known as the number one authority on the mustard family. Most of his early research was focused on weedy mustard species. With the exception of the grass family, this group contains more weeds than any other plant family. In addition to dealing with introduced weedy mustards, he was also working with a number of weedy native mustards and other related plants in the same genus that weren't weedy. So in an effort to understand the relationship between weedy and non-weedy, introduced and native mustard species, he gradually became interested in other genera such as *Arabis* and *Draba* that have many mustard species.

In the 1950s when my father was starting out, no one in Canada working in botany was even thinking about hybridization (the crossing of plants of different species). He was the only one to do so. He soon started to get a reputation, especially outside of Canada, as the Canadian expert on hybridization.

The two genera, *Arabis* and *Draba*, my father studied a great deal, had been studied by many others before him. However, his predecessors had just looked at the morphological characteristics (form and structure) in sorting out the genera.

My father comments, "When they would run into trouble, they would blame the confusion on hybridization." This was reflected in many textbooks that reported that one species would hybridize with another, making it difficult to sort out variations. Once my father became interested in studying *Arabis* and *Draba*, he collected plant specimens, grew them in the greenhouse from seed taken off the collected plants, got them to flower, looked at the chromosomes and artificially hybridized a lot of the species. My father reports, "These were wild species that had never been grown in a greenhouse setting and certainly had never been hybridized. By doing this, I found that in most of my crosses, the F1 hybrids were sterile. Therefore, all this information in the literature about variation being due to hybridization was wrong. Because they were sterile, there were no F2 hybrids or back crosses." Because of this work, my father discovered that the way to tell hybrids in the field is to determine if they were setting seed. This was a big breakthrough for anyone interested in these genera.

To make it even more complex, some of the species were found to be apomictic, meaning they produce seed without fertilization, in other words, virgin birth. By growing all these species and by looking at their chromosomes, my father was able to figure out this complex puzzle. He says, "A lot of taxonomy is the classification of organisms based on what plants look like, their morphology. Therefore, if you have plants that do not produce sexually, it causes all sorts of problems. But if you know what the mechanism is, it helps." And it helped him classify these genera. He knew how they were reproducing because he had grown them all in a greenhouse.

It sounds simple to say that my father grew all these plants. In reality, he had a lot of trouble germinating them. He had to give them cold treatment, he had to scarify the seed and then grow the plants. He found that most of the plants did not grow without vernalization (cold treatment). My father also had many challenges with the greenhouse staff. "They were used to growing plants from cuttings or from seed that germinated right away. These plants had to be babied." As a result, he ended up having to do a lot of the work himself.

☙ April 12, 1977 – It looks as if alternating temperatures are the answer to germinating *Draba* seed.

In the mid-1960s, my father undertook some work for Erling Porsild, a botanist and head taxonomist with the National Museum, currently known as the Museum of Nature in Ottawa. Porsild, born in Scandinavia, was famous for his youthful adventures following reindeer across the arctic. He was considered a Canadian authority on all sorts of arctic plants. His brother, R.T. Porsild, who worked in Yellowknife, would regularly collect arctic plants and send the material to Erling at the Museum for their collection, considered the National Vascular Plant Herbarium. At that time, scientists at Agriculture Canada had little to do with scientists at the Museum. However, my father used to go there from time-to-time to identify plant material for them. He became quite friendly with Erling Porsild. Porsild knew that my father had expertise in handling and germinating the seeds of arctic plants. One day he said, "I'm getting all this material from my brother and a lot of it has seed in it." Porsild was interested in getting chromosome counts of a range of arctic plants. He asked if my father would try to germinate some of the seeds and make chromosome counts. Ever the affable guy, my father said "Sure." So my father went through the plants, collected seeds, germinated them and made chromosome counts. He and Porsild coauthored three small papers together concerning chromosome counts of arctic plants.

About this time, Porsild telephoned my father to say that one of the Museum's geologists, Richard Harrington, had collected seed from a lemming burrow at Miller Creek, Yukon. A lemming skull found in the burrow was dated as being 10,000 years old. Porsild and Harrington thought that some seed found in the burrow was of a similar age. The seed looked quite viable though some had tooth marks on them. Porsild thought they were seeds of Arctic lupine (*Lupinus arcticus*). Harrington wondered if the seeds were viable enough to germinate. Porsild asked my father if he would try. My father did, and the resulting plants were indeed Arctic lupines. He brought the potted plants over and presented them to Porsild. The next thing my father knew, there was a paper written by Porsild, Harrington, and Mulligan published in *Science* about the germination of these 10,000 year old lupine seeds. My father comments, "No one had consulted me about this paper. Many people have asked me if I really thought the seeds were that old. I always said that I didn't feel the work was done in a scientific manner." All he could say for sure was that the seeds he was given had germinated and that they were lupine seeds. There was always the possibility that another lemming had recently used the same burrow and deposited the seeds within a few years of when they were discovered. In the 1960s, you could not date a living seed, so there was no way to confirm the age of the seed. This was a very popular story, picked up widely by the news media. The situation was an ongoing aggravation for my father, because he always doubted the validity of the information and was uncomfortable with his involvement in the story.

In 2009, Grant Zazula, a scientist working for the Yukon Paleontology Program of the Government of Yukon, Whitehorse, was able to obtain some of the seeds from Richard Harrington. Zazula and Fiona Brock, an expert in radiocarbon dating, from the University of Oxford, in the United Kingdom, were able to date the seeds accurately. They were found to date back to between 1955 and 1957. My father was not surprised by this. He is glad for this opportunity, finally, to clarify his role in this incident. He knows some people have probably always wondered about it.

When my father first started working on *Draba*, Porsild, along with some botanists from Northern Europe and Russia, were the main researchers of that species. Erling Porsild was one of the few people that my father thinks could properly identify arctic species of *Draba*. However, Porsild didn't have a standardized method of doing so. Porsild did have a plant key, but when my father examined it, it did not work. My father determined that it was because Porsild did not actually know the morphological characteristics of *Draba*. He explains, "Porsild was a field botanist, who had extensive experience observing and collecting *Draba* in its natural habitats. So, he could look at plants and identify the different species." It took my father quite a while to figure out that the descriptions and keys had nothing to do with how Porsild identified *Draba* species. He says, "The problem with *Draba* is that a number of the species grow together in the same habitat, so that often when the plants are collected, more than one species is collected. I have come across sheets of *Draba* in the herbarium that have multiple species on the same sheet, with all of them labelled as the same species. Sometimes a label did not correspond to any of the species on the sheet." In the early years, because there were not any plant keys for the species and because people talked about hybrids, when my father first started looking at these sheets, he didn't know what was going on.

People often collect plants and send them to my father because he is the specialist for the genera. He comments, "People used to send me their whole herbarium of the mustard family and want me to identify them. I continued to do a bit of this immediately after I retired, but it got to the stage where I was spending all of my time identifying other people's specimens." He tried charging per specimen to discourage people from doing this, but it didn't work. People would get grants and would be willing to pay him to do the work for them. "Now, I have a criterion," he says. "If they think that they may have something extraordinary, I will have a look at the specimens to see what I can do with it. If I'm interested in it, I'll work on it." Since he started doing this, he has found that most of the material people send to him is of interest to him. Annotating a specimen certifies that G.A. Mulligan, an authority on this genus, thinks that this specimen is this species. "Annotating can add value to the specimen depending on who made the identification," my father explains.

 ✍ April 5, 1982 – Had 4 sets of identification for *Draba*. One of over 80 specimens. I seem to be identifying all Canadian *Draba* and those of Alaska and Northern U.S.

My father explains the process, "When I examine a specimen and decide that it is a certain species, I use an annotation label or slip to identify this, for example, *Draba kananaskis* determined by G.A. Mulligan, plus the date. This label is placed on the herbarium sheet. It gives my opinion of what the species is. A specimen sheet could very well have several annotation labels put on by people over the years. I am having great difficulty right now with *Draba*. As I mentioned, I have sometimes found up to four species on one sheet. In such a case, my annotation label indicates species a, b, c and d. Each of the different species would have to be identified with my name at the bottom of the sheet."

Even in 2010, my father was germinating some seeds of a *Draba* species collected by Derek Lynch, a Quebec botanist. Lynch collected the seed in an area of northern Quebec that is not mountainous, but is located at quite a high elevation. The area is home to many plants also found growing on the high arctic islands. Lynch tried to germinate the seed himself, without success. My father says, "Arctic and alpine plants have to be handled in very particular ways to get them to germinate. The alternative is to collect actual plant specimens in the field." Lynch sent the seeds to my father. He had them growing in three pots on a shelf in the garage of his home, watering the seed every now and then. He placed them in the garage because he wanted them to have fluctuating temperatures. It does not break dormancy simply to put them in a refrigerator. Under natural conditions, the temperature goes up and down compared to the constant temperature in a refrigerator. In addition, arctic alpine plants do not grow very fast. He did not expect to get plants until the summer of 2011, and then he would have to give them some type of cold treatment to simulate permafrost conditions.

Lynch was very excited that it might be a new species of *Draba*. He and his colleagues were all waiting for my father to name this species. My father knew they were anxious, but he wanted to understand the species fully before he named it. He explains, "I was not prepared to rush the process. Naming a species to my satisfaction would typically take two to three years. I don't name a species until I have germinated it, grown it, and examined the pollen mother cells to see what the chromosome count is." At the time he speculated that it would probably be a diploid (2n or two chromosome sets in each cell), but wouldn't know for sure until he had fully examined the resulting plants. "I need to describe it properly and find a suitable Latin name for it," he says. A botanist gets to name a species when he identifies the plant as a new species. The person who found it, in this instance, knew it was a *Draba*, but not what type. As it turned out, sometime later, my father reports that the seeds in the garage did not germinate. He thinks the seeds were likely too old to be viable.

When a species is named, the species is described and a holotype is designated. My father explains, "A holotype is a specimen on a herbarium sheet, and usually contains one or two plant specimens. The name of the new species is attached to the plants on the sheet. It doesn't matter what is written about the holotype, the plant itself is the key piece of information. A researcher wanting to know about a plant will often go back to the holotype as a point of reference."

A perfect illustration of how complex this can get is a specimen sheet in the Biosystematics Research Institute herbarium my father was showing to one of the young scientists in early February 2011. The sheet was derived from specimens my father had borrowed from a herbarium in Geneva forty-five years ago. When the borrowed species was originally described, the person who described it didn't indicate a holotype. My father says, "It turned out that among the specimens on the sheet, I found four different species. As a result, I requested all the related species from Geneva that this person had worked on." My father then looked at the author's original description, compared it to all the specimens, and decided that the one that best fit his description was on one particular sheet. This particular plant then becomes a lectotype. "The curator in Geneva gave me permission to take a portion of the lectotype for the Department of Agriculture herbarium (DAO). The portion returned to Geneva is the lectotype; the portion I retained for our herbarium became an isolectotype. The Ottawa sheet includes the letter from the curator giving me permission to take it. You have to fold back the letter to see the specimen underneath it. Now anyone who writes on this plant uses that name and says, lectotype selected by G.A. Mulligan and then gives the reference to the resulting paper I wrote."

My father's college roommate, Paul Aird, told me that one of the things that really impressed him was when he heard that someone had named a plant after my father. In 2009, Ihsan Al-Shehbaz, a botanist working at the Missouri Botanical Garden, named an Alaskan species of *Draba* after him, *Draba mulliganii*. It is the only plant species named after my father. Paul Aird considers this the pinnacle of success. My father looks at it the other way around: "For me, the pinnacle of success is being the person to recognize a new plant species and naming it for someone else."

On reflection, my father feels that one of his most significant scientific contributions, and the one he received the most mileage from, was determining the chromosome numbers of plants. Generally, with some exceptions, an organism has a certain number of chromosomes and they are a certain size and configuration. Chromosome numbers are probably the most important single characteristic defining a species, but it cannot be taken as absolute because in certain cases the same species may have several chromosome numbers. It is however, a very useful tool. My father was not the first scientist in Canada to use this tool. This distinction went to two other scientists in their Institute: Dr. Ray Moore and Dr. Wray Bowden. Their interest was related to only a few plants. Bowden was interested in *Lobelia* and Moore worked mostly on *Caragana* and *Buddleia*. My father was the first one to use this tool extensively in Canada.

One of the things that my father undertook for the National Museum of Canada was identifying all their specimens in the genus *Arabis*, another mustard genus on which my father has written. My father started working on *Arabis* long before he began work on *Draba*. He was doing chromosome counts on *Arabis* and the chromosome counts he was getting were different from the counts published by Reed Rollins, with the Great Herbarium at Harvard University. Rollins was a very good authority, having published a comprehensive book on mustards of North America. My father used to correspond with him. They would send material back and forth. As a tribute to him, my father described and named a species, *Physaria rollinsii*, in his honour. However, it turned out that the chromosome counts that Rollins reported on *Arabis* weren't made by him; Dr. Lulu Gaiser (1896–1965), a botanist at McMaster University, completed them. She was considered a good cytologist (a biologist who studies the structure and function of cells). My father found that all of her chromosome counts were wrong for *Arabis*. He was able to determine that most *Arabis* species were apomictic (producing progeny without fertilization) and that many were also triploids (having three sets of chromosomes instead of two). Most triploids are sterile; however, if they are also apomictic, they can reproduce. Gazer did not realize this, so she was getting some odd chromosome counts. She was using the root tips; with this technique, she would only be able to see vaguely if there were a lot of chromosomes, or more, or less. The base number for all European species of *Arabis* is x=8, so they were either counts of

16, 32, 64 or some multiple of 8. With these poor preparations, if she saw something with a low count, she would say it was 2n=16. When my father started looking into this very early in his career, he discovered that all North American species have a base count of x=7, so they are either 14 or 28. There are also triploids that are 21. Gaiser was unaware of this, so she reported counts based on European species.

Although my father made many interesting counts that led to this discovery, he only published a couple of them because a new, younger scientist, Dr. Theodore Mosquin, joined the Plant Research Institute in 1963. At the time he arrived, Mosquin was working on *Arabis* and he made it very clear that it was his genus. My father had many other genera he was interested in, so he just moved on to *Physaria* and *Lesquerella*. However, much to his annoyance, although Mosquin collected a lot of material and made some chromosome counts, he soon became interested in *Linum* and dropped *Arabis*. My father would return to work on *Arabis* many years later, after he retired, as part of his research as an Honorary Research Associate.

Dr. Ihsan Al-Shehbaz has recently put *Arabis* in another genus, based on the chromosome work my father did that showed that most of the North American *Arabis* have a different base number than the European ones, while others match the European ones. While my father has great respect for Al-Shehbaz, he is not supportive of the reclassification of *Arabis*. Al-Shehbaz has used DNA information to decide that some of the North American species in the genus *Arabis* should be transferred into a separate genus. This means changing the name of about one hundred and fifty species. He has also transferred about three hundred species in the genus *Lesquerella* to another genus, *Physaria*, which has only about fifteen species. Al-Shehbaz then becomes the new authority for all of these hundreds of renamed species.

My father has articulated his concern about this type of

reclassification to his immediate colleagues, Paul Catling and Stephen Darbyshire, but since he is no longer very involved in the wider scientific community, his opinion has not gone beyond this limited circle. He states, "I do not agree with it. It is a game." He goes on to explain, "There is an international organization located in Belgium responsible for nomenclature rules for plant taxonomy. The rules of what people can do and can't do are published in *Taxon*.[2] There are several scientists whose whole careers are based on the transfer of names. These people get many publications out of doing this. Many people think this is great. It is a way to exponentially increase their publications, the almighty goal in science."

Looking at the issue on a broader scale, my father comments, "This is all further complicated by the fact that some botanists don't pay attention to or recognize these name changes. You therefore end up with publications using different names. Worse than that, when they change the name of a very important economic plant, it fouls up literature searches. All sorts of information is missed when only the new name is used in a search." In his opinion, these name changes should not be allowed. "There is a rule in zoology, and there are a lot more genera in zoology than botany, that if a name has been used for more than thirty years, you cannot change it. With so many more animal species, changing species names would lead to absolute chaos. This same rule should apply to botany," he says.

DNA isozymes are the current focus of quite a number of scientists that my father knows. However, he has been around long enough to see many things come and go. My father comments, "When I first started, people weren't looking at chromosomes, crosses, F1 hybrids, pairings of chromosomes and other similar relationships, but as the years went by all of these new ideas and the techniques to study them came on the

---

[2] *Taxon* is the bi-monthly journal of the International Association for Plant Taxonomy and is devoted to systematic and evolutionary biology with emphasis on plants and fungi.

scene. It used to be that a species was just a static thing. Then it became known that there were all sorts of ecotypes within a species responding to a tremendous variation in geographic growing conditions." He goes on to say, "The classification of plants is a tool to understand the relationships between plant species. At the time of Linnaeus, everything was based on what plants looked like, their morphology. Now, it has gone to the other extreme, with some botanists figuring that all they have to do is DNA analyses to determine a plant species. When they get differences in DNA they name new species." Clearly exasperated, he says, "It has been proven over and over, as information has been revealed and then superseded by yet newer information, that this approach does not stand the test of time. A technique such as DNA analysis is just another tool and should not be considered in isolation as a source of definitive answers. A broader knowledge of the species is required to figure things out. One should not be blinded by any one technique and ignore everything else."

"A piece of work done diligently and methodically a hundred years ago, read today is just as likely to have good and valid observations and conclusions now," my father states. When he was starting out as a scientist, a famous case provided a cautionary tale: a scientist couple, Áskell and Doris Löve, who focused their research on chromosome counts. "Based on their research, if you had a difference in chromosome numbers, it was determined to be a different species. Based on this thinking, they changed the names of all sorts of species. They had a huge following. It was proven eventually that what they were saying was incorrect. Getting a different chromosome count does not mean it is a different species. In addition, a lot of their data is absolutely useless now because it was found that they manufactured a lot of data to justify their work."

Internationally, many people know my father only as an authority on weed biology and weed systematics. He is known as the weed man. This is because my father is a cofounder and long-time editor of *The Biology of Canadian Weeds Series*, which documents all biological information known worldwide on Canadian weeds. Paul Cavers, a professor at the University of Western Ontario, originally proposed this series. After Cavers arrived from England, he founded a school of weed biology at Western. Cavers had many graduate students and he wanted to start compiling information on Canadian weeds. He approached my father and asked him to become involved. Then just as they got started, Cavers took a one-year sabbatical in England. My father decided to go ahead and prepare the outline for the series, which asks various questions about each weed. Even though Cavers initiated the idea, my father was the one who got it off the ground.

My father and Cavers completed some of the weed profiles, but others contributed, including some botanists from the United States. Since 1973, over one hundred and fifty accounts have been published in *The Biology of Canadian Weeds*. In order to get the series published, they approached the *Canadian Journal of Plant Science* and managed to get them to agree to publish it as part of their journal. Their agreement was conditional on them getting someone to quality control the submissions. My father became the first editor of the series while Paul Cavers took the lead in finding authors and tracking their progress. My father ended up reviewing all of the submissions made for the series until he retired as Director of the Biosystematics Research Institute in 1987. When he did, he turned over the responsibility to Suzanne Warwick. My father laments, "This turned out to be a mistake. She used the position mainly to further her own career, not in the best interest of the publication." Paul Caver took it over in the end. My father says, "I regret not turning it over to Cavers or one of his students to start with. They were better qualified." He had been Director of the Institute for many years, and he was conditioned to looking after the interests of the Institute first and foremost.

In 2013, in acknowledgement of the fortieth anniversary of the publication, Paul Cavers and Stephen Darbyshire co-authored a history of the series, with input from my father. They report, "The series was popular from the outset, in fact there was such a great demand for many articles that the authors' stocks of reprints soon were exhausted. In 1979, Agriculture Canada published a book containing the first thirty-two accounts in the series. Gerald Mulligan was the editor and compiler. In 1984, a second volume containing the next twenty-nine accounts, with the same editor/compiler and publisher, was printed. Volumes 3, 4 and 5 were published with Paul Cavers as the editor/compiler by the Agricultural Institute of Canada in 1995, 2000, and 2005."

In their nomination letter for the Lawson Medal, Darbyshire and Warwick stated, "In a career spanning more than fifty years, Gerry has made a substantial contribution to many aspects of botanical science both in Canada and internationally. Not only have his contributions been as a researcher, but also as a prominent figure in the Canadian and international science community in administrative and leadership roles." Not a bad scientific legacy for someone who had to fight so hard for the right to be allowed to do research.

7
BIGGEST PROFESSIONAL INFLUENCES

The biggest single influence in my father's professional life was, without doubt, his first boss at Agriculture Canada, Dr. Clarence Frankton. Frankton had a significant early influence on my father's career. He was the person responsible for really getting my father started as a botanist.

In the course of going through my father's diaries, there is a 1976 entry in which he very proudly documents the receipt of notification that two of his research papers had been "accepted as is" by the *Canadian Journal of Botany*. While my father does acknowledge that does indeed indicate a well-written paper, he stresses that it was a very long road to get there. "It was not easy. Writing did not come naturally to me. It involved plain hard work to get there."

My father attributes much of his becoming both a good writer and a good reviewer of scientific papers to the training he received from Clarie Frankton. "Frankton was an excellent writer and editor of the *Canadian Journal of Botany*. He knew the value of words and he was a very insightful person," he says. The other key contributor to his growth as a writer was once again his habit of seeking out and studying examples of successful paper writing by top scientists from around the world.

In January 2013, my father paid homage to Frankton by naming a species after him. My father had been working on some research with Ihsan Al-Shehbaz, from the Missouri Botanic Garden, when he proposed the name *Draba franktonii* for a new species. In making the recommendation, my father told Al-Shehbaz, "Clarie Frankton was Secretary General of the Montreal International Botanical Congress, had a distinguished career as a weed taxonomist, and was the person whose support and friendship was of prime importance throughout my career." Al-Shehbaz's immediate response was, "A well-proposed name. I have admired your collaboration with him on several weedy genera since my early days as a graduate student."

As my father grew as a scientist, a trio of his peers most strongly influenced his thinking. Jim Calder, Roy Taylor, Keith Jones, and he used to have frequent discussions on all the latest concepts in biology, as well as the latest developments in taxonomy and systematics. They did this during the period that Jones worked at the Institute from 1958 to 1959. It was a true meeting of the minds. Scientifically, they were his most important influences.

Jim Calder (CEF[3] 1946–1966) was a good scientist who knew a lot about botany. He is considered one of the best plant collectors in Canada. His career was limited by his lack of a PhD. Unlike my father, Calder did not actively pursue pushing the boundaries. My father found this very unfortunate. Jim Calder ended up taking early retirement in 1966 at the age of fifty-one. My father paid tribute to this friendship and his great respect for Calder by naming two species after him, *Lesquerella calderi* (G.A. Mulligan) in 1969 and *Arabis calderi* (G.A. Mulligan and Porsild) in 1995.

---

[3] Central Experimental Farm.

Dr. Roy Taylor (CEF 1957–1968) and my father shared an office for several years. After Clarence Frankton retired, Roy Taylor became the new Section Head. Dad says, "Roy was a good scientist, who kept up-to-date. I feel that it benefitted my career, working with him." In his turn, my father played an instrumental role in Taylor pursuing a new career path. Shortly after Taylor became Section Head, a position became available at the University of British Columbia Botanical Garden. My father says, "Roy was very interested in the position, but it was only an assistant professor position. He was not going to apply." My father encouraged his friend to apply for the job. He said, "Tell them what your qualifications are, that you are interested in the job, but will only take it if you are made a full professor." Taylor applied and, in 1968, got the job at the rank of full professor. He was Director of the UBC Botanical Garden for seventeen years, then Executive Director of the Chicago Botanic Garden, one of the largest gardens in the world, for nine years, and finally Director of the Rancho Santo Ana Botanic Garden in California for the five years before he retired. As it turns out, sharing an office was a fortuitous paring for the both of them. In May 2013, Roy Taylor died. My father was very upset on hearing this sad news of the loss of a special colleague and friend. Again, my father paid tribute to a valued friend and colleague by naming a new species after him, *Draba taylori* (G.A. Mulligan and Al-Shehbaz) in 2013. In communication with Roy's widow, Janet Taylor, my father told her, "I consider Roy to be one of the kindest and most helpful people that I have ever known. He was not only exceedingly generous, but was an inspiration to me."

Keith Jones (CEF 1958–1959) was a visiting post-doctoral fellow who came to Canada from Wales. After returning to Britain, he eventually became Assistant Director of Kew Gardens, followed by Director of Jodrell Laboratory in London, one of the biggest and most important laboratories in Europe. In 1982, on a visit to London, Jones and his wife took my father and mother on an amazing tour of the city thanks in part to

Jones' also being an authority on the history of London. He has always remained a good friend of my father's. They have met up at several conferences over the years, where they usually found time to have a meal together and to catch up on each other's lives and careers.

The four colleagues not only worked well together, but also played well together. They regularly played poker and went to Ottawa Rough Riders football games together. My father and Taylor even won the Civil Service Recreation Association Curling Championship together, two years in a row. My father comments, "This was very unusual because we had to beat a lot of teams throughout the public service to do so." The four had a unique and close friendship at a key time in my father's career. In recounting this time, my father speaks very fondly about each of them.

8
STUTTERING

"I'm a stutterer. I have been a stutterer, as long as I can remember," my father says. His stuttering really bothered him growing up. He didn't like to get up and talk in class. "There were a lot of things that I might have done, that I didn't do, because of my stuttering. I definitely feel that it inhibited me when I was young," he says. One of the things that he found particularly difficult to do was talk on the telephone. Many times, he opted to walk miles and miles to go and talk to someone in person rather than telephone him or her.

Stuttering is genetic. It is inherited. Quite a few members of my family have problems with stuttering, with varying degrees of difficulty and duration. Given how many current family members have a problem with stuttering, it seems likely that this must run in the family. When I ask my father about this, he is quick to agree. "My cousin, Earl Cain was a stutterer. I think my Dad was too." My mother agrees. Dad goes on to say, "I also think that one of my Uncle Nelson's sons was a stutterer. All the members of the Mulligan family that I know of who stuttered, other than Robyn (granddaughter), were male. It probably went back in the Mulligan family for many generations. There was a predisposition to it. How each person was affected by it and handled it depended to a great degree on his or her personality."

My father had a bit of a problem with kids teasing him about his stuttering when he was young. He started school at a younger age than his peers so he was always the youngest in the class and therefore usually the smallest. This, along with his stuttering, made him a target of bullies. However, my father proudly comments, "Bullies certainly found out fast that if they tried to push me around, I could take care of myself. I always had the idea that it was better to face up to them, even if I ended up with a bloody nose. I realized very early that all bullies, if you were willing to fight them, quickly moved on to easier targets who wouldn't push back." He feels that he is lucky because he is a fighter so bullies became wary of him. My father's athletic ability also helped him since he always hung out with a sports crowd, who were often a lot bigger and stronger than those inclined to tease him. His teammates looked out for him.

Paul Aird, my father's roommate at Macdonald College, also remembers that talking on the telephone was a particular problem. "He certainly did stutter a lot," says Aird. Aird wanted to help his roommate whenever he could. He launches into a story: "Guys talk about a whole lot of things and occasionally, they talk about girls! During one of these talks, I found out that your father was interested in asking your mother, Margaret McDonald, out to a movie. However, with his stuttering, phoning her presented a problem." He and my father got together and planned that Aird would call on his behalf. Aird says that they discussed it in a fair amount of detail. They used a pay phone outside of the university residence.

When Aird called the women's residence and asked to speak to Margaret McDonald, the response was, "Who's calling please?" After he told them it was Paul Aird, he could hear the person who answered call out "Margaret McDonald, phone call from

Paul Aird," thereby ensuring that everyone in the residence knew about the call. When my mother came on the phone, Aird told her that Gerry was with him, but was having difficulty with his stuttering. He wanted to invite her to a movie on Friday night. Aird does not remember what she said, but he transferred the information on to my father. "We had arranged to have Gerry say something to Margaret after she agreed to the invitation," he says. Aird comments, "Gerry was petrified of speaking on the telephone. This is my one clear memory of him trying to deal with his stuttering on the phone. I have never forgotten it."

Great story, from my point of view, but when I recount it to my parents, they both vigorously deny it. My father says that there is no doubt that he was petrified of speaking on the telephone, but maintains that he definitely made the call himself. My mother agrees. She knows it was him, because my father's voice is so distinctive. Dad remembers, "Shirley Palmer, a student I knew, was on the switchboard that night. She called up to Marg." My mother came down to the telephone and he talked to her. That's how he remembers it. They went to a movie together, *An American in Paris*. My mother pipes up saying, "It was a good movie." Unbeknownst to both of them, the title character in the movie was a guy named, Gerry Mulligan.

Aird says that he just accepted his roommate's stuttering. He did, however, always wonder how he managed to be so successful at work when he couldn't handle talking on the telephone. What happened was, in 1953, my father had just graduated from Macdonald College and was working at the Central Experimental Farm in Ottawa. He read an article in *Maclean's* magazine profiling a professor at the University of Toronto, Dr. Ernest Douglass, who was working with stutterers. My father talked to his boss, Clarie Frankton, about Douglass. He told Frankton that he found it difficult to get up and talk at meetings. He really wanted to go to Toronto and take a course with Douglass. Frankton could see that this was important to my father, so he agreed to give him leave without pay to enable him to do so.

My father travelled to Toronto to take the course, held at Douglass' Bloor Street offices. There were others taking the course with him. In the end, the course did not offer techniques on conquering or minimizing stuttering that my father had hoped would solve his problem. Instead, Douglass' main message to participants was this: if you're a stutterer, you aren't going to get rid of your stutter. The real problem for stutters is that they don't want people to know they stutter, so they avoid doing things. Douglass tried to drill into the class that stuttering was an affliction and they should just go ahead and get on with things. "If you don't worry about it and you get on with your life, it gradually won't bother you and won't become a problem for you." As part of the course, Douglass would put them in groups and send them out onto Bloor Street to stop people on the street and talk to them, in other words, confronting a stutterer's worst nightmare.

The course was a real revelation for my father. He definitely felt it was worthwhile. However, it wasn't what he thought it was going to be. He had hoped that it would provide a miraculous cure. What he did learn was the very valuable lesson of not avoiding doing things he wanted to do because of his stuttering. The message was to make the best of it. As a result, my father started to speak up more. He stammered, but came to realize that that's just the way it was going to be. "It released me from having to worry about it," he says. Soon after he finished the course, he had a prime opportunity. My parents were married within the year. My mother recalls that he spoke at their wedding and did very well. "It was a real test for him."

Later, as more research was done on stuttering, my father came to understand that stuttering is caused by seizing of the vocal chords. The more nervous and worried about it you are, the more they seize up. A particular technique my father likes to use to control his stuttering is to try to fool his vocal chords or throat into thinking that he is not going to speak, that he is just going to breathe. This prevents the vocal chords from seizing up. Many stutterers also tend to speak faster than they should. Slowing down your speaking is beneficial for stutterers.

> ✍ September 12, 1991 – I obtained a book from the library on stuttering suggesting using a slight exhaling of breath to relax the vocal cords before speaking and speaking first word slowly and then a comma or a long first word in two slow syllables.

One of the other methods my father has used in overcoming a verbal block is word substitution, "Before I went to Toronto, I would substitute a word or idea if I felt a block coming on. This often meant that I would end up saying something that I knew was foolish. I always felt terrible about this. After taking the course in Toronto, I became determined not to make substitutions, but to say what I meant to convey even if it meant that I stuttered. To my amazement this resulted in less anxiety, and in turn less stuttering." The revelation of not giving in to a source of stress taught my father a valuable lesson that he says has served him well throughout his life. It was central to his decision as a manager not to sanction or take part in any dishonest directive, even if he was ordered to do so by a more senior manager. Because of this, he is able to say, "I found my time as a manager very enjoyable and not particularly stressful."

When my father took the course in Toronto, he had just graduated from university, so he had no money saved for the course. Nothing was paid by Agriculture Canada. During the six months that he attended the course, he says that he had to work three terrible jobs to pay for the course and his room and board. One of those jobs was working at St. Lawrence Corn Starch as a bagger. He also worked for a furniture refinisher. As part of that job, his hands were exposed to many strong chemicals. He finally ended up working for the Defence Research Board taking care of research animals such as orangutans, dogs, cats, and many white rats. He liked that job in some ways because he enjoyed feeding the animals and cleaning their cages. However, he was disturbed by the physical damage to the animals. He says, "Some of the animals were really vicious because they were being traumatized. You had to be very careful around them."

Coincidentally, my mother was living in Toronto during the period my father attended the course. Although I teased him about it, he swears that it was not the motivation for him taking the course. On graduating from Macdonald College in dietetics, my mother was required to complete a one-year internship at a hospital to become a dietician. She was actually accepted at hospitals in both Vancouver and Toronto. Vancouver was her preferred choice, but her father felt that it was too much money. The internship was an unpaid position. Room and board were included, but travel and other expenses were not. My grandfather decided that she should accept the one in Toronto. My mother says, "I think that if I had gone to Vancouver, I might never have come back. A friend of mine, Helen Stewart, went and she never returned and has never attended any of the reunions."

My father comments, "We went together during our last year in university. She was my girlfriend. When we graduated and I came back to Ottawa, I visited her in Montreal. Toronto is a lot further away than Montreal. I might not have seen her during the year she was interning. It was by chance we both ended up there at the same time. I didn't go to Toronto to be with her. I went seeking help with my stuttering. I felt that my career was being jeopardized because I was terrified to get up and saying anything. It didn't solve my stuttering problem. It solved the problem of my being terrified of getting up, of avoiding situations. That was the big lesson."

During the time they were both in Toronto, my parents were able to see each other every night. To minimize costs, my father stayed in a rundown room on University Avenue. Their budget only allowed them to eat at the cheapest restaurants they could find. The time they spent together in Toronto solidified their relationship. If my grandfather hadn't intervened in my mother's decision of where to intern, I wouldn't be here. In fact, it was during that August, after the wedding of my mother's best friend and cousin, Liz Gareau, that my parents got engaged.

By that time, my father was back working in Ottawa. My mother took a one-week holiday from the internship program. The wedding was in Cornwall, with my mother's whole family in attendance and my mother acting as maid-of-honour. After the wedding, they all returned to the McDonald cottage on the St. Lawrence River. My mother and father went out for the evening by themselves to the nearby village. My father took the opportunity to give my mother a ring and they became officially engaged. My mother pipes up, "I loved it! It was beautiful." My father says, "It wasn't a surprise proposal. When we were both in Toronto, we had talked about getting married and we had discussed what kind of ring she wanted. We even did a bit of ring shopping." My father goes on to recount, "I will always remember, we were all sitting around the breakfast table the next morning when I thought, she hasn't told anyone." He was surprised and disappointed. Then suddenly, my mother's sister, Janet, noticed, "Margaret, you've got a ring on!" My mother very casually commented, "Yes, I got engaged last night." My father finally got the reaction he had been expecting when he first came down.

The 2010 movie, *The King's Speech* captures very well the sheer terror that stutterers experience trying to speak in public. My father believes he could never have been a Director or Acting Director General if he had not taken Douglass' course. As a senior manager, he had to speak at many meetings, during many high-pressure situations. It eventually reached the stage where doing so didn't bother him at all anymore. "As you accomplish things, you become more and more confident," he says. It obviously worked. Rosanna (Menchini) Carson, my father's executive secretary when he was Director of the Biosystematics Research Institute, says, "While I did notice Mr. M's stuttering, it never bothered me. It was that way from the beginning and that's the way it was." It was never an issue among staff as far as she knew.

In talking with Paul Aird, I was also interested to hear that his exposure to my father's stuttering had a lasting impact in how he dealt with other stutterers whom he came across throughout his life. In one instance, when Aird was teaching in the Faculty of Forestry at the University of Toronto, he had a student who stuttered. The class was required to make a presentation and normally this person was exempted from having to fulfill this requirement. Aird approached the student and asked him to try to make the presentation. He invited him to come to his office and make a dry run of the presentation, speaking only to him. "This one-on-one presentation went so well, that the student agreed to make the presentation to the entire class," he says. When Aird thinks about it, he is brought to tears at how well it worked out. "He made the presentation, and his fellow students were so pleased for him."

In another instance, Aird tried several times to arrange for a forester from the Ontario Ministry of Natural Resources to present to his class. Aird felt that this person, well along in his career, had a lot of knowledge to give to his class; however, the person stuttered, and had repeatedly declined all of his invitations. Finally, Aird managed to convince him to make a presentation. Again, it went very well.

The family member with the most severe stutter is my niece Robyn, my oldest brother Don's daughter. When the whole family gathered in Perth, Ontario in the fall of 2011 for the wedding of another niece, Sheree (my brother Steve's oldest daughter), I decided to interview Robyn. I went prepared, but was uncertain whether the right circumstance would present itself to conduct the interview. As it happened, there was a two-hour gap between the ceremony and the reception. I was one of the few people in my family who had decided to stay overnight in Perth after the wedding. As a result, I had a room at the only major hotel in town. In a completely unplanned fashion, both Don's and Paul's families all ended up in my room during this period. I decided to seize the opportunity.

I had no idea how Robyn would respond to speaking about her stuttering, especially as it turned out, in front of eight other members of her extended family. But she was thrilled to be asked. "Very few people ask me directly about my stuttering. I wish more people would be more forthright in addressing the elephant in the room." We all learned so much from her, and for her part, she found out for the first time that other family members also have problems with stuttering. The other nieces and nephews were entranced by the whole conversation.

Right from the beginning, Robyn made it clear that she doesn't think of her stuttering as a problem. She was also delighted to hear about her grandfather's philosophy of learning to live with stuttering and responded with a heartfelt, "Great! I don't normally meet other people who have a stutter. In my whole life I have maybe met two people who stutter." Since *The King's Speech* movie was released, Robyn has had a lot more people ask her questions about stuttering. While she welcomes the direct approach, she says, "I still don't always know the best way to address other people's reactions to my stuttering. A lot of people make fun of or mimic a stutterer."

My Dad comments, "Robyn has a much more significant stutter than I ever did" and he thinks himself the second worst stutterer in the family. He hypothesizes that the severity of Robyn's stuttering may be linked to physical development problems related to her premature birth. Robyn weighed only two pounds, six ounces when she was born. My father says, "I got around stuttering a lot by avoiding the situation. Robyn doesn't avoid it; she goes in headfirst. Her stuttering may be more obvious because she talks more. She is such an outgoing person." My grandfather coped by not talking a lot. This characteristic quietness of so many of the males in my family, in fact, may be tied to verbal communications problems. It is a way of avoiding the problem. If you don't speak much, it reduces the problem.

Even while recognizing that she is an outgoing person, Robyn says that she gets many comments along the lines of, "Oh, I would have expected you not to want to talk in front of people and not to want to be around social scenarios. In university, professors were always apprehensive about asking me to speak, thinking I wouldn't want to talk. I never let that hold me back. I was even a guest lecturer. Once when I was in class making a presentation worth about half my grade, I just could not say the name of the researcher who was the subject of my talk. I could not say her first name for the life of me. I was able to say her name twice, but then started to stutter and by the fourth time I could not get it out. I finally just said, 'Yeah, you know who I mean.' The whole class burst out laughing. I was outside the norm for a stutterer. People always seem to think that stutterers are super reclusive." Based on all the male stutterers in our family, I remind her that that assessment isn't far off the mark. While not reclusive, most haven't been big talkers. Robyn chuckles, "I just talked a lot from a young age."

I also stuttered for a while in Grade 1. At the time, my two oldest brothers and I were attending a French school some distance from our home. Often my father would drive us to school. For a short time, he also picked up another young girl attending the same school who made fun of me. My father noticed the effect this was having on me and stopped driving her. I have no recollection of this. I still have a minor problem stuttering, but only in high tension situations. I had a recent run in with a contractor on one of my construction projects. He was aggressively trying to get additional money by claiming unauthorized extras. He was getting angry and started shouting at one of my colleagues, accusing him of lying. This did not go over well with me. In responding to his behaviour in an emotionally charged atmosphere, I got stuck on a word. As I was struggling to get a word out, I could see him enjoying my dilemma. I quickly switched the word I intended to use and proceeded to tell him that his behaviour was unacceptable and if he continued in the same manner, the meeting was over.

In July 2012, my parents and I visited my brother Don and his family at their weekend home in Canmore, Alberta. Robyn was living there and working as a manager in a local coffee shop. Knowing what kids are like and remembering hearing about the problems she had in school, I was particularly interested in the nasty topic of teasing. "Yes, I was teased. The worst teasing was by kids in grade school. It started to taper off a bit in grade seven or eight, although I had an especially hard time between the ages of twelve and sixteen with girls being mean to me. I constantly felt on the outs of whatever group I was in."

I am surprised by this. Robyn always seemed to have many good friends. "Yes, I did," she confirms. The problem was that she had a few friends from many different activities — soccer, ultimate Frisbee, field hockey, dance and art — but none of these pods of friends overlapped. So the normal structure of high school, where you have a large group of friends who would move through your classes with you and stand up for you didn't happen. She never benefitted from the peer support that my father had received. She says, "I did not have that protective group that prevented people from going after me. If you are perceived as a person on your own, or part of a smaller group, you are an easier target I guess." When I tell her, that I am like her in that I have always had a few very good friends from the different parts of my life instead of large groups of superficial friends, this gives Robyn pause. "I always attributed not wanting to be in large groups to be a consequence of my stutter, but it could just be part of my personality," she says.

I am curious. I never found my father stuttered very much at home, certainly much, much less than the stories told about him by others. I ask Robyn if she finds that she stutters less when she is with people she is comfortable with. Her initial response is an enthusiastic "Yes!" and then a qualified, "For the most part. I also stutter less when I know what I am talking about or when I am excited about something. At the beginning and end of my thought process when I am talking or when I am about to read something I stutter for the first few sentences and the last few. Once I get into the pattern of speaking its easier. It's a type of rhythm. It's the same reason why you don't stutter when you sing." All of her close friends have told Robyn that after they have known her for a while, they forget that she stutters, until someone else points it out. Other people will ask her friends about her stuttering and how they should address it. They have told her that they are always surprised, "Oh yeah, I guess she stutters."

It wasn't just Robyn's peers who gave her grief. "I also had a few issues with teachers in high school," she says. I am incredulous on hearing this. One instance sticks out in her mind. "I once had a substitute teacher outright mock my stutter in front of the class. Thankfully, I had a friend who was great. After class, she went up and talked to the teacher. I didn't want to. I thought, you know what, she's not going to be here for long, so whatever."

I ask Robyn if the teasing hurt her, or if she just reached a point where she accepted it. "I was hurt by it for a long time. I already had low self-esteem, so being teased and harassed so much and for such a long time just further contributed to the problem," she says. After telling her about her grandfather's approach to dealing with those harassing him about his stutter, I ask if she ever tried to stop the teasing. "No. I didn't try. I just walked away." As my father predicted, the passive approach puts you at risk of being considered the easier target. Unfortunately, an aggressive, defensive approach is not within everyone's makeup.

"When I was about sixteen, I started to get over it, to not be as affected or hurt by the teasing," Robyn says. It wasn't until a few years ago, in her early twenties, that she has been better able to cope with people's reaction to her stuttering. I find this interesting because it is almost exactly the same age as when my Dad took his course in Toronto, which completely changed his attitude to dealing with his own stuttering. I suggest that as they both matured, they gained confidence and learned to cope better with the situation. For Robyn, the key was when she truly started to realize it was the other person's problem, not hers. "I also realized that I was smart enough to surround myself with good people who weren't going to make an issue of my stuttering. In elementary school and high school the pond is smaller and you are forced to be friends with whoever happens to be there," she says. In other words, the wider world provides a bigger pool from which to select.

That said, Robyn still struggles to know how to react when she is teased or mocked. One of the problems is that stuttering isn't as common as many other afflictions that are targets of ridicule. She suggests that people therefore don't know how to respond to it. "I find some people at work, in the service industry, will mimic a stutterer without even being aware that they are doing it." As a result, she tries to look for the intent of people's reaction. Is it a mean-spirited poke or an unconscious one? She tries to respond according to the intent behind the comments. Robyn also cites her strong family support as an important factor in helping her deal with prolonged bullying. "I learned to persevere. It would have been even more difficult without them," she says. Perhaps being so badly teased is a big contributor to Robyn being such a caring person, so sensitive to other people's needs, I suggest. Robyn vigorously agrees, "Yes! That is very, very true!"

When we visited Robyn in Canmore in the summer of 2012, she and my father chatted about their mutual experiences with stuttering on a walk together along the Bow River. She told him about the problem she has being in groups and trying to speak. "I don't like talking in groups. I start to stutter and because I am not speaking loud enough, someone else invariably starts to talk. By the time my word gets out, I end up talking at the same time as someone else who thinks that I have finished speaking. It makes for many awkward moments — do I talk, do I not talk scenarios. Usually, I just stop talking. It's not worth trying to get control of the conversation again. Quite often, when I try to say something, nothing actually comes out. A few people paying attention will notice and ask if I want to say anything. So, I prefer being in a smaller group."

Robyn has also learned the same key lesson as my father. "Mainly for me, I try not to allow it to dictate what I do. At university, I have been a guest lecturer and I have spoken at conferences. I feel that it's go two feet in or don't go at all," she says. When I ask Robyn if this was a personal revelation of her own or if she got advice from someone on this outlook on life, her response is "I may have. I wasn't that old when I took stutter therapy. I have gotten worse in the last few years, likely from the stress of university. In university I have had to do a lot more public speaking." She does admit though that the main ramification of her stuttering is that it shifted her career goals. "I have been told I would be a good teacher. My interest would be to teach at the high school or college level. Unfortunately, I know how brutal high school students can be to any teacher who is different. They were relentlessly teased. With my stutter, I know I would be a target. I accept this. It is what it is."

I observe that the speech therapist to King George VI of Britain in the movie *The King's Speech* seems to have focused mostly on breathing techniques to help the King overcome his stammer. Robyn says, "Yes, when I was involved in early speech therapy, breathing exercises were part of what I was taught. From what I understand about the way I stutter, when I try to talk, the air escapes and my vocal cords close down. I was taught to breath out and then start speaking, so there is no possibility for my vocal cords to close ... in theory anyway." Her mother, Sharon, says that Robyn probably doesn't remember some of it because she was so young, but over a two-year period, she had to practice diaphragm breathing every day. But Robyn does remember. She says that even now, when she stutters she automatically puts her hand on her stomach to cue the breathing technique. By putting her hand on her stomach, she can feel the progression of her breath and know when to breathe out or to talk.

Robyn was in grade two when she started speech therapy. "They were clear that it wasn't going to fix the stuttering," says Sharon, "it was just going to help her manage her way out of it. If you really concentrate and try to manage it before you talk, you can prevent the stuttering, but it takes a tremendous amount of energy to do this. They don't encourage you to be that extreme, just to think about what you are doing. If you practice, practice, practice, it becomes entrenched and you can actually do it to some extent without thinking consciously about it. It makes you less likely to get into trouble. It takes years of practice. It's a real commitment. Robyn made that commitment."

One of Robyn's main techniques for dealing with her stuttering is that she changes words in her head before she says them. She had never heard about anyone else doing this. She is surprised and interested to hear that her grandfather does the same thing. Robyn says, "A lot of my close friends think it is hilarious when I get caught on a word like 'coat'. I will try about five times to get the word out, and then suddenly I'll switch to 'jacket'. They will laugh and say they all knew I was going to say coat."

I mention that Dad had also learned from Dr. Douglass that there is such a thing as interiorized stuttering. Apparently interiorized stutterers use classic avoidance techniques in such a way that most people are completely unaware that they are stutterers. Interiorized stutterers use physical ticks or distinctive body movements as a way of overcoming a verbal block. My middle brother, Steve, does this. I had never known or made the connection between his body movements and stuttering. It was just something Steve did. Apparently, my nephew Dale, my bother Paul's oldest son, does this as well. His mother, Carol, pipes up with the observation that Dale has such physical mannerisms. His brother Kevin concurs. Dale used to stutter when he was younger. Robyn is just amazed to hear this: "Really! How did I not know that?" Dale interjects that he still sometimes loses words.

Robyn recounts a series of day-to-day situations that can cause stutterers problems. "My stutter is why I don't like to go to Starbucks or Subway. You have to make eight different verbal decisions. I just want a coffee! I don't want to have to say eight things to get one. I also hate ordering food over the telephone." She relates a story that she says is funny now, but at the time was really frustrating and upsetting. She was living in a Kelowna residence at the University of British Columbia's Okanagan Campus when she tried to order some Chinese food over the telephone. "I was really stressed out with mid-term exams. I could not get my words out. The woman on the phone did not speak English well and she kept saying, 'Sorry, you are breaking up.' I tried to say no, I have a stutter, but she said, 'Hold on, just hang up and call back.' So I called back and I could barely get anything out again. She says, 'Give me your number, I'll call you, your phone is still breaking up.' I was trying to say, 'Oh no, wait no, but...,' then she interrupts saying, 'Oh, I don't need it, we have it here.' So she hangs up and calls me back. I did not pick it up. I decided that I did not want Chinese food that badly. At the time, I was almost in tears. It was ridiculous. Eight, nine times I tried, on every single word."

On the disturbing side, Robyn tells us, "One of the things that happens a lot to me when I go to a restaurant and have trouble stating my order, the server treats me as though I have a low IQ. They bend over and talk to me as if I'm five years old. 'Oh, sweetie, what do you want? Do you want this?' I'm thinking, 'Really! I do speak English!' I even get this when I am ordering alcohol. I have learned to be amused by it."

I always wondered what the difference was between speaking on the telephone as compared to speaking face-to-face. Robyn explains, "It is the stress of thinking people will misinterpret what you are saying. If I am talking on the phone, it is one less avenue I have to get across what I am trying to say." I comment, "You must like text messaging." "Yes, a lot," she says. I am sure that texting would have come in very handy for my father as well. Some people will comment to Robyn, "You don't like to call, do you?" "No, I prefer to talk by text," she says, "...or Skype, because you can see the person. It makes it easier." Carol asks, "So seeing someone's face makes it easier?" Robyn responds, "If they can see me, they can see if I am having problems speaking. They know it's not a bad connection."

Listening to Robyn, I am amazed at the things you just don't even think about. I ask her how she copes when she calls a number that requires endless voice commands to navigate to what you want. I tell her about a recent experience I had where none of the options were what I needed. I got so fed up, I screamed in frustration into the phone. After a pause, the voice calmly responded, "I'll connect you to an operator now." She vigorously agrees that they are a big problem for her too. "Did you say...? No, I didn't say that."

Repeatedly, Robyn's great sense of humour and friendly, outgoing personality have helped her not only cope with her stuttering, but flourish as a young adult. My already high opinion of my niece just soared into the stratosphere after I talked to her about stuttering. What a girl! I tell Robyn that she has impressed the hell out of me with how well she has dealt with all the harassment she has been subjected to over the years. I am especially in awe of the fact that she has no lasting bitterness toward all the people who have hurt her with their taunts and insensitivity. I don't think I would have done as well. Robyn is appreciative of the compliment. In fact, both Robyn and my father have coped remarkably well with something that would have brought many other people to their knees.

These long overdue discussions within our family about stuttering have been a real revelation for many of us. My sister-in-law Carol, a grade school teacher, comments, "This is all good information for me." I wish we had thought to do this sooner. It is my sincere hope that the stories of how Robyn and my father have dealt with their stuttering provide some positive and instructional information to other stutterers and those who interact with them. I consider them both excellent role models. I also hope that those who encounter someone in the future with a stutter will be more understanding and supportive in how they react because, in the end, this is the greatest challenge that stutterers face.

9
FIELDTRIPS

A big part of being a botanist is frequent summer fieldtrips to collect plant specimens. My father's first opportunities to do fieldwork were when he was a technician for Dr. Clarence Frankton. Frankton didn't like to stray beyond the Ottawa district, so my father was able to obtain some great experience by undertaking the more distant fieldwork.

Once my father graduated from university, he started to carry out his own fieldwork, typically with the assistance of a technician. This fieldwork extended throughout Canada and the United States, including a lot work in remote alpine areas. This resulted in many challenging and adventurous experiences.

Technician Cliff Crompton was a frequent assistant on my father's early fieldtrips. In November 2010, I contacted Crompton to obtain his input. In a return email to me, he shared, "Gerry M. and I worked together for many years. He was one of my first supervisors when I became a permanent employee at the 'old' Plant Research Institute, Weed Investigation Unit under Dr. Clarence Frankton. I sort of feel that I know you, as Gerry always kept us informed of you and your siblings activities, all good I may add." Unfortunately, any further opportunities to obtain Crompton's insights were lost when he died unexpectedly in the fall of 2012. I am sure he knew a lot about us, as we did about him. When you spend a whole summer together in the field, there would be lots of time to share the details of each other's lives.

In addition to collecting plant material, there were many shared adventures. My father recounts, "One time Cliff Crompton and I were driving on an alpine logging road in the southern part of British Columbia. It was near lunchtime. We had brought our lunches with us, so we decided to pull over on the side of the road to eat. Well, it was lucky that we did, because not long after a huge logging truck came roaring down the mountain at full speed. If we had still been on the road, there was no way that it would have been able to stop. It scared us badly. Shortly after, yet another truck sped past. We flagged one of the drivers down and asked him how they knew when to use the road. He told us all the truckers had walkie-talkies. This allowed them to coordinate their use of the road, a one way road."

"Another time," my father tells me, "in southern Alberta, near Coleman, our map showed a road through Kananaskis to Banff. Cliff and I decided to use this road to travel to our next collection site." However, they didn't know this road was a high country road that was closed most of the year. "We started up the road and only realized we had a problem when we were quite high up. At that point, there was no place to turn around, since there was a sheer drop on one side. It got so bad that the truck started to slide on the muddy road. We didn't know what to do. I said I would drive, if Cliff would push the side of the truck to keep us from going over the side. So we crept slowly along. When the car started to slide, Cliff would push the car back onto the road." Once they were finally up and over to the other side of the mountain, Cliff asked, "What were you going to do if it started to go over the side?" My father's jovial reply was, "The whole way across I was primed to jump out of the truck." My father goes on to say, "Cliff did not seem to appreciate this strategy."

In yet another instance, this time in Montana's sagebrush country, my father says, "I once stepped off a big flat boulder right onto a rattlesnake. Even as I saw it, I couldn't stop myself. I actually stepped on it. In those days, we didn't wear protective footwear. I was just wearing my normal Hush Puppies. I reacted by jumping up in the air; luckily, the snake did not strike but just took off. That summer, Cliff and I saw quite a few rattlesnakes."

Snakes were one of two major hazards of working in sagebrush country. The other problem was ticks. This is the habitat of *Physaria*, a group of plants in the mustard family, the plant my father was collecting. My father tells me, "At the end of each day, we would have to examine each other for ticks. They would be right underneath the skin. We would find them on a fairly regular basis. If you tried to pull them out, you could leave the head buried in your skin. To get them out we used some of the chemicals we had on hand, fixatives for preserving plant cells. These chemicals were typically alcohol and formaldehyde. We would take one of these chemicals and put some on the rear end of the tick. This caused it to back out. We would then pick it out. Ticks carry Rocky Mountain Fever. It is deadly. We worried about this a lot on fieldtrips."

Many of the plants my father studied were alpine plants, growing above the tree line of mountain ranges. "Something that got me into trouble several times was the collection of *Draba* on almost vertical faces," he says. "I would spot a plant twenty feet above me. I had no problem climbing up to collect it, but often I couldn't get back down. It is a lot easier climbing up because you can see all your handholds and footholds and pick them out. But once you are up there, clinging to the side of the rock face, you always wonder how you are going to get down." This begs the question, "If you as an accomplished athlete had trouble collecting in this type of terrain, what do scientists do who are not as agile?" My father responds, "They don't go on fieldtrips within such challenging terrain. They would tend to pick species to study that do not grow in difficult habitats."

My recollection is that my father would take off on a fieldtrip every second summer. I don't remember missing him greatly, because we had grown up with him doing this. I do remember being very excited to meet him at the airport when he returned. In those days, the Ottawa Airport was a very small facility. You could virtually greet the person as they stepped off the airplane. I have vivid memories of him returning from a fieldtrip to the United States with three felt cowboy hats for my two older brothers and me. My mother thinks I would have been around five years old. There was a black one, a red one, and a white one. The red one became mine. I loved it!

By contrast, I also remember that my mother did not always handle my father's prolonged absences well, particularly when crises arose, such as one of us getting hurt. My father agrees, "When you kids were young, Margaret found it difficult when I went on fieldtrips. She rarely complained about it. One of the few exceptions was when I returned from a two-month fieldtrip to Colorado. When I got off the plane, you were all there waiting for me. I was so happy to get home and see the family. However, the first thing my wife did was pour out all her troubles. It was just like someone had dumped a bucket of cold water on me." As a result, as my brothers and I got older, my father didn't go away for long periods. When we got old enough, the whole family started accompanying my father on his summer-long fieldtrips. These became much treasured family experiences.

The first family fieldtrip occurred in 1967 to collect *Draba* along the Gaspé Peninsula. My three brothers and I would have been between the ages of five and twelve years old. Fred Beales, a technician, and his wife Ruby were also part of this trip.

The Gaspé trip did not work out quite as well as my parents had hoped. The plan had been for the family to camp during the trip. The very first day, it poured rain the entire time that my parents tried to put the tent up, and in those days' tents that would hold six people were not easy to put up. My father remembers, "To compound the problem, we put the tent up in a hollow. All the rain ran right into the tent." It was the first and last night that we camped. From then on, we stayed in cheap motel cabins. This worked out well, especially because it continued to rain frequently. Part of the cost of the trip was covered by Agriculture Canada. My father had a certain amount of funding to work with, and he was very careful in working out the costs. "We really worked hard to do things on the cheap," he says.

Fred Beales and my father would head out each morning to do their fieldwork. On one excursion, they found a caribou antler on Mount Saint Jacques, the highest peak in Quebec. The family would spend the day around a succession of cabins. There were a lot of black flies and no-see-ums to contend with that summer. We kids were fascinated by Fred Beales' frequent stops for Coca-Cola. My mother was not as thrilled about it, because we all kept bugging her for a Coke too.

My middle brother, Steve, has memories of the Gaspé fieldtrip, mostly of the constant travelling. His favourite memory is playing on the beach and especially making driftwood forts. "It was an adventure," he says. My youngest brother, Paul, is not too sure if his memories of the Gaspé trip are his own or if they stem from looking at all the family photographs. "I was very young. I think I have a clear memory of the driftwood fort and Percé Rock, but maybe they are just memories from the photographs." I find it interesting that all three of my brothers have cited the forts as their strongest memory of that trip. For myself, I remember shell handicrafts made by the locals and wading through tidal pools rich in sea urchins, starfish, small shrimp-like creatures, and many different types of seaweed. To this day, that summer is the most fascinating and fun shoreline experience that I have ever had.

In 1969, the whole family again accompanied my father on a fieldtrip, this time to the Rocky Mountains. This turned out to be the trip of a lifetime for our family. It was a great adventure and it was the last big family trip before our summers started to be taken up with summer jobs.

By this time, my parents were better able to afford a family fieldtrip. What influenced the decision was that Ted Mosquin and his wife had stayed in Banff National Park the previous year on a fieldtrip. Mosquin arranged with the federal Department of Forestry to stay in a cabin for the summer. My father was still working on *Draba* and wanted to do some collecting in the western mountains. He says, "When I heard about the potential availability of a forestry cabin, it appealed to me. We would be able to stay right in Banff National Park." So my father applied to stay there and received approval. When my mother was arranging for airline tickets for herself and my brothers and me, they found out that it was much cheaper to book the tickets privately than through the government travel bureau. For that particular trip, it was twice as much. My father decided to book his flight privately as well when he realized the huge difference.

The log cabin was located in the middle of Banff National Park, near Mount Eisenhower, later renamed Castle Mountain. It was a forested area, with a cabin backing onto Altrude Creek. The family fished in the creek every day for brook trout. Virtually every morning we ate pan-fried trout for breakfast. My brother Steve has fond memories of both the cabin in the woods and in particular fishing in the creek all the time.

On this fieldtrip, the entire family accompanied my father on about eighty percent of his field expeditions. We climbed many mountains that summer. *Draba* is a species found above the tree line. In typical style for my family, it became a competition on every climb to see who would be the first one to spot *Draba*.

Everyone learned to identify *Draba*. The shout of "Draba, Dad, Draba!" was often heard that summer.

It was an accident-prone summer. Steve was injured twice; I was injured once. We became very familiar with the Banff hospital. The first time, Steve was speared with a fishhook. We had been fishing and Don's fishing line got tangled up in Steve's fishing line. In the ensuing mess, one of the fishhooks went right through Steve's finger. Steve remembers Dad saying, "That's okay. I'll just take my pliers and cut if off and push it through." Steve says, "When he touched the finger, it hurt like hell, so I yelled, no way!" At the hospital Steve comments, "Actually, they did the same thing. Of course they froze the finger first."

The second time was during a fieldtrip to a restricted mountain area that my father had access to as a federal government employee on business. He had a key to the gates to allow us to drive up to an alpine meadow. This is also where we found a big horn sheep skull. Don and my father were climbing up the mountain, while the rest of us stayed down in the meadow. Steve, Paul, and I were playing around in a rocky area. The rocks were really sharp. Steve fell and cut himself badly on one of them, necessitating another trip to the hospital for stitches.

I was injured when my brothers and I walked from the cabin site to a nearby village. Our destination was the local corner store for popsicles. As we were crossing the TransCanada Highway overpass, I tumbled down one of the interchange slopes and landing on probably the only piece of broken glass in an otherwise pristine Park. Trip number three to the hospital.

Paul was still pretty young during the Banff fieldtrip. Again, he wonders if the pictures reinforced the experience for him over time. "I have often wondered," he says, "why I remember more about the summer in Banff than many more recent summers since then. I have concluded that it is because it was such a departure from what we normally did. It was also so well reinforced with periodic slide shows and the repeatedly told family stories."

One of those family stories is how we almost lost seven-year-old Paul on one of our mountain climbs. We had hiked many miles into a mountain area where we then began ascending one of the mountains. We were about halfway up the lower slope. The climbing was difficult, largely consisting of scrambling up a loose talus slide. At one point, we were strung out across the slope, but headed toward a small clump of trees. Just as most of us had reached the clump, a part of the talus slope began to give way, right where my youngest brother Paul was standing. Luckily, my Dad was right near him. Just as he was starting to get swept away, Dad reached out and grabbed him. After the initial shock, my mother's classic response was, "Let's eat!" So we did. With one hand on a tree, we all proceeded to eat our sandwiches and carrot sticks. My mother has never lived it down.

One of Paul's favourite memories is swimming in Altrude Creek. The water was frigid glacier runoff. Being young and resilient, we used to slide down the creek rapids behind the cabin. The cold would numb us so we wouldn't feel anything skidding over the rocks.

Fourteen-year-old Don worked as my father's assistant that summer. The few times that the two of them went botanizing alone, it was usually when there was a more difficult climb. Don worked hard carrying the plant press and backpack. "We had a routine," he says. "Dad would collect the plants and place them in the plant press. Then he would pick some young buds and pickle them in acetic acid." Dad explains that the buds were necessary to look at the pollen mother cells under the microscope. This is how he determined their chromosome counts. Don comments, "To this day, whenever I smell vinegar, I think of that summer." Don remembers it as a positive experience. He is sure that he developed his love for the mountains that summer. He remembers hiking above the tree line with panoramic views of the surrounding mountain peaks. He enjoyed the physical challenge, searching for *Draba* and spending time with his father in the middle of the mountains. He does not think it a coincidence that he ended up living in the mountains, in Canmore, Alberta.

Whenever possible, we tried to maximize the use of gondola lifts or forest access roads to reach as high as possible, and then walk the rest of the way up. Don's strongest memory is the ordeal of the expedition up, or more precisely back down, Rogers Pass. Rogers Pass is located in British Columbia, near the Alberta border. This area is known for its huge amount of snowfall, with thirty feet per year common. All this moisture produces lush vegetation, including huge trees. Don wanted everyone to know that they didn't really get "lost"; they just strayed from the route they had taken up the mountain. Both Don and Dad maintain that they always knew where they were because they could see the valley bottom. On the way down, they ended up walking through a draw with a tremendously dense alder thicket. Don recounts, "It was like a jungle, except worse, because instead of leafy vegetation it was little spindly twigs. Unfortunately, I made the mistake of wearing short pants that day. When we finally reached the bottom, I looked down at my legs. They were scratched to pieces, everywhere. I didn't wear short pants again for the rest of that summer." On another difficult expedition, the two of them met some mountain climbers well outfitted with special climbing boots, pants, and walking sticks. As my father and brother looked down at their own regular clothes and Hush Puppies, they both thought, "What are we doing here with these people and all their equipment?"

One of my father's colleagues, Jack Parmalee, a mycologist (a scientist studying fungi), and his family did the same trip that summer. They stayed in a forestry camp in Kananaskis country. At one point during the summer, the two families switched places for a few days. This allowed my father to do some collecting in the Kananaskis area. Their cabin was located on a former temporary military base. All the buildings were white and surrounded by highly manicured lawns, quite the opposite to our rustic cabin in the woods.

The Parmalees also visited us in Banff National Park. They had been playing cards when my father tried to get Jack Parmalee to have a beer. Jack declined because they had to drive back to Kananaskis that evening. On the way back, their station wagon hit a moose. It absolutely demolished the car, but thankfully no one was injured. When Parmalee called to report the incident to my father, he commented, "If I had had that beer I would have been in real trouble. I'm so glad I didn't." My father laughed and said, "Jack, if you'd had the beer, you would have been later and you wouldn't have hit the moose!"

Don recalls the Kananaskis climb when they found a plant they thought might be a new species of *Draba*. Most of the *Draba* they had seen had white flowers, but this one had light yellow flowers. Steve and I found an old tin kettle in a midden pile at the base of valley. We used it to pot up a live plant specimen of the new species to take back home. We transported it by hand on various laps on the airplane ride back to Ottawa. I wonder how the current airport security procedures would respond to such a carry on package. These days, you would never be able to get something like that through security.

My father says that when you describe a new species, you have to validate it by indicating the type specimen, you have to write a description in English and Latin, and you have to publish it in a recognized journal for the name to become valid. "From then on anybody who doubts it and thinks it was related to something else would have to borrow the holotype, which we collected, and look at it to see how it compares with what they have."

Scientifically, for my father, the discovery of *Draba kananaskis*, a new *Draba* species, was a minor achievement. Its importance is personal, because it was found during a fieldtrip on which his family joined him. The type specimen is in the National Herbarium and the authority is G.A. Mulligan, with the collectors listed as G.A. Mulligan and D.G. Mulligan. It was collected during the time the family stayed at the Kananaskis forestry station, found on the eastern slope of the Kananaskis Range near Snow Ridge Ski Resort (now Fortress Mountain Ski Resort) twenty-five miles south of Highway 1 (the TransCanada Highway) on Kananaskis-Coleman Road (now Highway 40), at an elevation of 7250 feet.

More extensive collections of *Draba kananaskis* were made a few years after the initial discovery by Dr. C.C. Chinnappa and his students from the University of Alberta in Edmonton. They went to the site and gathered quite a bit of plant material, as well as taking many photographs of the species. Some of the specimens and photographs were sent to my father and have been included in the National Herbarium. The bulk of the material is part of the University's collection.

My brother Don has souvenirs of that pivotal summer, like the light green canvas backpack with leather straps that they used to carry specimens. It is mounted on the wall in his Canmore home. "If you compare it to the backpacks of today, you realize that it identifies that era, the 1960s. I also have a copy of the research paper published in the *Canadian Journal of Botany* that documented the new *Draba* species we found." My father recalls the green truck he drove that summer: "It had big doors at the back. It was a precursor of today's minivans. It was almost a delivery truck. There were only two front seats. You kids were sitting on loose grates in the back of the truck. You would probably be jailed now if you were ever caught doing that with your kids today."

Steve's wife, Susan, says that the trip was so memorable for him that they chose it as the destination for their honeymoon, in mid-August 1981. They stayed at the campground in the little village at the base of Castle Mountain. Steve interjects, "Actually, we only camped for one night. It was so cold we ended up staying in some nearby cabins instead. The water was frozen in the morning when we got up. That was a pretty good indication of how cold it was." Susan comments, "We assumed it was warm out west in August because it is warm in Ottawa then. We had to buy an extra sleeping bag." My mother sympathizes. "It's a lot colder, especially in the mountains. We got caught not having enough warm clothes on the 1969 fieldtrip." I remember it being really cold and windy on the top of the mountains we climbed. There is a classic photograph of the family huddled behind a makeshift stone fort on the top of a mountain.

Steve and Susan found the cabin we stayed in that summer and took a nostalgic walk along Altrude Creek. Steve says, "We fished. We caught brook trout. We also saw some bears." The bear that left the biggest impression on them was the one they spotted along the Bow River. They were strolling along the river, not far from their cabin, when they noted an area where the grass was all patted down. "We kept walking and were about a hundred yards past the spot when we looked back and saw the bear. We hot footed it out of there by scrabbling up the riverbank and heading straight for the car," he says.

The Banff trip was the last fieldtrip that included the whole family. My mother and Paul would have been the only participants in subsequent trips. My mother says, "After the Banff trip, your father did not make many more trips." And of course, after he became Director there were even fewer. Paul says, "The fieldtrip I remember best was the one to the Boston area. Dad was looking for the type of poison ivy that climbed up trees and hydro poles. It was classic Dad, stopping along the side of the road, everywhere!"

⌀ June 23, 1976 – Paul, Marg and I leave for east cost of U.S. on a *Rhus* field trip.

⌀ June 24, 1976 – I found various *radicans* on rocks back from beach.

⌀ June 25, 1976 – I went out alone in morning and found *Rhus* shrubs, 4 ft., climbing with aerial roots, up trees, telephone poles and boulders. Climbers to 1.5 inch diameter.

⌀ June 26, 1976 – Headed north and found a big stand of *Rhus* in New Hampshire. Traveled to Boothbay Harbour and then to Rockport. I found *Rhus* near Rockland and then more near cottage at Rockland.

⌀ June 27, 1976 – We left Rockport, Maine and drove through to St. Jean, Quebec. Picked up *Rhus* three times en route.

Paul also says, "It was the first time I had been to the United States. It was a big deal for me. I remember buying my first record album, by the Beach Boys. I was so proud because the Canadian dollar was worth more than the American dollar, about $1.06 US. I also remember being so disappointed when they wouldn't take Canadian money. They said, "What is this?" I was incensed. "What do you mean, what is that? It's worth more than your money."

This excursion was also distinguished as the trip where my mother suffered severe food poisoning. Paul recounts, "We were staying at a motel right on the beach. It was around the fourth of July. They had set up an enormous bonfire in preparation for the event. The night before, someone lit it prematurely. There was a huge fire. Dad thought the motel was on fire at first. He tried to get us both out, but Mom was so sick she moaned, "Just leave me, I want to die." Between the fire and the food poisoning, there was a lot of drama that night.

In July 2012, on a visit to Don's home in Canmore, Alberta, we had a taste of alpine botanizing forty plus years after the initial Banff adventure. My sister-in-law, Sharon, had the brilliant idea that Don and I accompany our eighty-four year old father on a helicopter excursion up to an alpine meadow on nearby Mt.

Charles Stewart. My father collected quite a few specimens that interested him. Once he returned home and had a chance to examine them in more detail, he reported that he had collected six mustard species (*Brassicaceae*), *Draba incerta*, *Draba crassifolia*, *Draba juvenilis*, *Draba macounii*, *Draba porsildii*, and *Smelowskia calycina* var. *Americana*. After looking at all the photos I had taken on the mountain, Sharon laughed and made the observation, "Anyone else landing high in a mountain meadow surrounded by stunning mountain scenery, would be looking up at the mountains. In every single picture you are all looking at plants on the ground." Some things never change.

10
BOTANICAL PHOTOGRAPHER

Much to the embarrassment of my brothers and me, my father is famous for pulling over to the side of the road in order to get out and crawl around on the ground taking pictures of weeds. On one occasion, this almost caused an international incident. My father was looking to take some pictures of cattails. He had seen some on Limebank Road and made a mental note of their location. Limebank Road runs along the southern edge of the Ottawa International Airport. In November 2004, he finally went back by himself to take pictures of them. He was sitting down on the side of the road, in the ditch, focusing his camera on a cattail. Suddenly, some shadows loomed over him and he heard a deep voice say, "What are you up to sir?" He looked up and there were two big RCMP officers standing over him. They repeated, "What are you doing there sir?" My father explained to them that he was just taking pictures of plants. "Well, I think you had better move along sir." They didn't explain, but they seemed to mean business, so my father decided to comply and left. He was amazed that they followed him for quite a distance. They obviously wanted to make sure he was gone. Later that day, he found out that President George W. Bush was arriving at the airport that day, just about the time he was in the ditch. RCMP and Secret Service Agents were probably all around the airport looking for suspicious people. I guess a seventy-six year old botanist sitting in a ditch qualified.

My father's photography of plants dates back to quite early in his career. It was not something many of his colleagues were doing. He just had a personal interest in taking photographs, and he applied this interest to his work. His first camera certainly wasn't a single-lens reflex camera. "I couldn't see what I was taking a picture of through the shutter. It was especially difficult to take a close up picture of a plant," he says. To allow him to do so, he made a wire frame and mounted it on the front of the camera to help frame the picture. It also had to be centred to make sure that you actually captured the plant. His second camera was better, but still a no-name brand. He used this camera extensively to take pictures of plants in the field. He comments, "I used government film, but my own camera, because Agriculture Canada would not provide me with a decent camera. I used slide film exclusively."

Unfortunately, on a fieldtrip with Ted Mosquin, collecting in the mountains of New Mexico, my father lost this camera. He had been taking pictures of plants prior to collecting and field labelling them. They were halfway down the mountain when my father realized he didn't have his camera. It was near the end of a long day of fieldwork. Mosquin asked, "Are we going to go back up?" My father responded that even if they went back up, they probably wouldn't be able to find it. He told Mosquin, "I'm so bloody tired, to heck with the darn camera." They figured that someday, someone hiking in the mountains of New Mexico would find a rusted out camera. So for some time he was without a camera as my parents could not afford to replace it. When my father looks back, it probably would not have cost that much to get another camera, but with a young family, it was a low priority. This is why there are so few pictures of my youngest brother, Paul, born in 1962.

My father eventually got a better camera, a Pentax, followed years later by an even better Pentax. Eventually, when he turned eighty, he made the jump into the digital age. He had been having health problems, with chronic pain habitually keeping him up most of the night. He was looking for something to focus on instead of his pain. My brother, Steve, helped him to buy a fairly sophisticated Canon digital camera. My father marvels at how difficult it was to get a decent picture in the early days compared to his digital camera.

After so many years of taking pictures, of course, my father has an extensive collection of botanical slides. "If I had stored the slides properly, they would not have deteriorated as much as they have. I had them in slide storage boxes located up on a cupboard shelf. Unfortunately, a lot of the early ones have lost their colour depth," he says. He is trying to replace as many of the plant photos as he can, because the quality that he can get with his new digital camera is far superior. He can also crop the photos in various ways. "It is a completely different ball game," he states. Since my father took his slides over so many years, and in every part of Canada, as well as many parts of the northern United States, he will never get the opportunity to take most of them again. As such, they remain an incredibly valuable resource. He didn't want them just to sit in boxes on shelves. He wanted them to be useful. In 2004, he started going through his slides and scanning them.

With these newly scanned photos, my computer savvy brother, Steve, a Data Warehouse Developer with the IBM Software Group, helped set up a website that was part of my father's Internet provider package. They put many of his scanned slides on the Rogers website. My father was gratified when the site proved to be popular and he was getting many visits. Unfortunately, around the twentieth of each month, access to the site would be denied with a message from Rogers saying it was getting too much traffic. My father was not very happy about this, because for the rest of the month the information became unavailable. Rogers wanted him to pay a lot of money for a website with more capacity. Since he was not making any money off the site, my father was not willing to do this. To add insult to injury, Rogers then decided to change their websites completely. Suddenly his web address changed. He had to start over, rebuilding his loyal following. "When the site was moved, it was never the same," he laments.

One of my father's colleagues at Agriculture Canada, Stephen Darbyshire, knew about the problems he was having and suggested that the Canadian Weed Science Society might be interested in hosting the site on their website. When the Society did indeed confirm their interest, it seemed like the ideal situation. My father and brother decided to take the opportunity, because the society website would offer a lot more bandwidth. Once again, in 2006, Steve set the site up. The society provided my father with his own web page on their website. This worked well for a long time, and the site was at the top of the list of several Internet search engines. The main problem with this site was related to my father's desire to make frequent updates and additions to the site's information. He had great difficulty dealing with the consultant responsible for the website. The Society was just one of the consultant's clients, so attention to changes was infrequent. The consultant asked if my father could make the changes himself. It sounded complicated, but Steve was willing to do it. The consultant ended up giving Steve the access code for the website so he could make the changes.

Eventually that consultant moved on to other things and responsibility for the site was taken over by a woman from Saskatchewan, who was a member of the Society. In the transition, my father's information was taken off the old website while the new site was being set up. My father kept sending emails asking when the information would be reinstated. It turned out that this woman was not able to do the work herself, she needed to rely on yet another person to do the work. The new website format would also change the location of his information. Steve explains, "Every time the location of the information is changed, you start all over again with Google and other search engines." This had already happened when the site changed from Rogers to the Canadian Weed Science Society. They found that it generally took about a year to return to a point where my father's website reached the top of a search engine again. At the point when the information had been offline for six months, Steve suggested to Dad, "Why don't we create our own website, rather than staying with Canadian Weed Science Society? They could do the same thing to us again."

In 2009, Steve did some investigating and found that they could get their own website for a hundred dollars a year. Steve's first order of business was to obtain a domain name for the site that wouldn't change. "We could then go from site-to-site, anywhere we wanted, and keep that name," he says. My father proudly reports, "When Steve picked the website name, weedscanada.ca, he was brilliant! If someone is interested in knowing something about Canadian weeds and type in 'weeds of Canada', my website comes right up, even without Google. In the category of common weeds of the northern United States and Canada, my website has always been number one out of eight thousand entries. I don't think there is any doubt that the name weedscanada.ca is responsible for this." From Steve's point of view, it means they finally have a stable website for as long as they want. He says, "The information on the new site is exactly the same, but the amount of bandwidth we have now is a lot higher. The new Internet service provider is used to hosting commercial sites with a lot of information. Also, because the new domain name is so short and simple, it comes up a lot faster on searches."

According to my father, "Before we used weedscanada.ca, we had a lot more American visitors accessing the site. About seventy percent of the visitors were American, with ten percent from Canada and the rest from a variety of other countries. Now, when Americans see Weeds Canada they tune out right away." Because he is featured on Google Canada, anyone in Canada interested in weeds and common or roadside plants will find his site listed first. Presently, some days about two-thirds of the people who visit the website are Canadian. Changing the name of the website changed the people visiting the site much more toward my father's target audience.

That said, his website is also featured on Google search sites for other countries. My father really enjoys tracking visitation to his website. Steve has made it very entertaining for him. My Dad tells me, "He has set it up so that I can see who is accessing the website, where they are from, and what information they are accessing. The flag of the visitor's country appears first. Frequently in the morning when I check the website, the flags of nine or ten different countries come up." Steve says, "Recently, I have seen the Netherlands, Hong Kong, India, France, Italy, Croatia, Australia, Hungry, and the Philippines."

My father finds many visitors from Canadian universities, the Ontario Agricultural College, Agriculture and Agri-foods Canada, the National Capital Commission, and the Department of National Defence. There is one organization that he particularly relishes visiting the site: "I get a lot of downloads from Agriculture Canada. They are on my website all the time retrieving information." On a year-round basis, he consistently records one hundred to two hundred visitors per day to his current website. It builds up over time, but every time the website changes locations, they have to find it again. At one time, he had over one thousand visitors per day. This daily count has been steadily increasing with the new name. As of March 2014, the total count is 638,000 visitors.

In setting up the new site, Steve retrieved all the information from the Canadian Weed Science Society. The society was not happy, but my father wanted more control over the site and a stable presentation of the material. In spite of everything, my father still maintains ties with the Canadian Weed Science

Society, which provides links to his website. He is constantly updating the material with new species and new photos. Although the original scanned slides looked good at the time they were done, there was a big difference when compared to the new digital photos. He is constantly on the lookout for the species that have poor photos, so that he can take new digital photos. On a regular basis, he provides Steve with a list of changes, so that he knows exactly what to do, which takes time. My father still wishes that he could make the changes himself; he always feels guilty about asking Steve to do the work for him.

My father's first web presence was actually a popular bilingual Agriculture Canada website on poison ivy, poison sumac, and western poison oak. As usual, there was some reworking of the website and the information disappeared. My father got in touch with one of the managers at Agriculture Canada to ask if he could do something to get it back online. The manager said he would look into it after he returned from vacation. When my father contacted him again, he found out that this manager had been seconded to another position. At this point, my father gave up, recreated the information, and put it on his weedscanada.ca website. He used his own photographs and rewrote all of the text.

My father actually now has five websites:

- Common weeds of the northern United States and Canada (weedscanada.ca)

- Common plants of the northern United States and Canada reported to have caused poisonings, dermatitis, or hay fever in humans (weedscanada.ca/poisonous_weeds.htm)

- Plants of the northern United States and Canada reported to have caused poisonings to livestock or have tainted animal products (weedscanada.ca/plants_poisonous_animals.htm)

- Additional information on hay fever plants (weedscanada.ca/additional_hayfever.htm)

- Weedy mustards, *Brassicaceae (Cruciferae)* of Canada (weedscanada.ca/Weedy_mustards.htm)

Certain things are popular. The information on poison ivy is consistently popular. Steve says, "There are people coming from the Wikipedia page on Poison Ivy, which has a link to the Poison Ivy page on weedscanada.ca." In addition, when a plant is in the news, such as Giant Hogweed (*Heracleum mantegazzianum*), its information gets a lot of visitation. My father will often include something new that is topical. He will take a new picture, create a write up, and post it on the website.

Establishing and keeping a website is just as difficult and frustrating as trying to get his many books and pamphlets published. My father's hallmark, his persistence, once again has served him very well. He says, "Some people think I'm crazy, but it is a hobby for me. I enjoy it."

11
HEALTH AND SAFETY IN THE WORKPLACE

When my father was doing cytological work early in his career, his office was in a laboratory in the Botany Building, the brick building in the arboretum area of the Central Experimental Farm. "When I started to work on chromosomes, all the chemicals I used to process the material for microscopic observation were stored in the same room as my office," my father says. Three of the solvents he used in carrying out this work were xylol, dioxin, and formaldehyde. All of these chemicals are now known to be highly toxic to humans, with a wide range of health effects including neurological and carcinogenic.

My father describes the situation, "There was a terrific odour in the room. I used to get physically sick. I really didn't feel well for the four or five years that I was in such prolonged and close contact with these chemicals. In those days, we didn't have any protective apparatus such as fume hoods or other ventilation systems to protect us. We didn't even know about them."

I consulted my sister-in-law, Sharon Mulligan, an industrial hygienist and until recently Director of Corporate, Environment, and Health and Safety for Petro Canada, about what she knows about the chemicals my father was exposed to early in his career. She says it's difficult to determine what effect they have had on his long-term health. "You can have short-term symptoms without long-term effects and, vice versa, have long-term issues without any short-term symptoms. If he had things like dizziness and headaches, that would reflect a systemic response. He might have inhaled the chemicals. What people don't realize is that skin absorption can be even more detrimental to your health than inhalation. Whether the chemicals were absorbed into the skin depends on if he wore gloves or not. Often a person's nose is so sensitive it protects you by warning of exposure to chemicals. When you smell something, you self-correct your behaviour to avoid the smell. If it smells bad, you get outside, into the fresh air. Dealing with skin contact is not as straight forward and people tend to forget about it."

Sharon goes on to say, "Effects depend on the volumes of the chemicals and how much time he was exposed to them. You can have exposures and not be that significantly affected, but have many short-term symptoms. But if he had a lot on his hands, with skin exposure, that would be as much of a concern as inhalation. The short-term symptoms tend to be associated with hydrocarbon type exposures. You tend to self-protect because you get headaches, you get a bad taste in the back of your throat. You get yourself out of the situation. Short-term impacts are warning signs that you are getting too much of something." When my father hears this, he immediately comments that, based on that thinking, probably the worst exposure to chemicals he had was when he worked for a furniture stripper in Toronto the year he took his course on stuttering.

Once my father realized what was happening, he wanted to get his office out of the lab. But where was he going to go? The solution to reducing his exposure to these chemicals started a whole chain of events that indirectly ended up with him becoming Director. "I wanted to move my office out of the same room where I conducted my research, but I still wanted to continue doing the work," he says. There were a number of other scientists in the same building. He asked one of them, who he knew very well, if he would be agreeable to him moving in with him and they could both use my father's office as the lab. My father was disappointed when this person turned him down. He didn't want to share his office. Fortunately, Roy Taylor heard about my father's problem and said, "Gerry, you can move in with me and set up the lab in your office. I have no problem sharing my office." The difference this made to my father's health was significant. "I immediately felt better. I have always felt very kindly toward Roy Taylor for being so generous," he says.

My father mentions two other scientists of his generation who did a lot of cytological work, Wray Bowden and Ray Moore, both of whom worked in similarly unhealthy circumstances. Both died young. My father has suffered from undiagnosed chronic pain for many years. He has sometimes wondered if his early exposure to such potent chemicals may have played a role. "I have no idea if exposure to these chemicals contributed to my present health problem. I do know that at the time they really bothered me," he says. When his former executive secretary, Rosanna (Menchini) Carson, hears about my father's chronic pain, she immediately suggests that the chemicals he used as a scientist may be the cause: "I have noticed that a lot of scientists have died of cancer."

His own experience in dealing with risks to his health in the workplace would forever make my father sympathetic to others with similar problems. Many years later, when he was Acting Director General, just before he retired, my father was in a position to help someone else.

∅ October 22, 1986 – I went in to the Director General's office and got updated on the problems connected with the disposal of toxic chemicals.

At one time, there was a Cell Biology Research Institute at the Central Experimental Farm. One day, two of the staff members working with radioactive material were asked to take some of the material and dispose of it. They put the material in a government vehicle and drove to the disposal facility. To their shock and amazement, they were met by people in full protection gear, including gloves. This scared them badly. They talked to the staff at the disposal facility, who told them, "You should not be handling stuff like that. It's radioactive and can cause all sorts of health problems." They went back and talked to their Section Head, inquiring, "What are you going to do about it?" Their supervisor was not willing to do anything, and neither would their Director. No one responded to their concerns.

One of them decided to take out a grievance to force Agriculture Canada to deal with his health and safety concerns. His grievance was against his Director, who brushed the grievance aside. So the union made an appointment with the Director General to discuss the situation. As soon as my father heard their story, his immediate response was, "You're kidding me! I grant your grievance and, as a matter of fact, I order your Director to rectify this situation immediately. I want this looked into and for you to be properly equipped." The union representative couldn't believe what he was hearing. What he didn't know was that my father had once been in a similar situation with no help. It had never entered his mind to grieve his own problem. He just tried to resolve it himself.

12
THE ETHICAL MANAGER

My father had no grand plan of becoming a manager. "It happened gradually. If an opportunity presented itself and I thought I could do the job, I tried it," he says. When Roy Taylor left to take a position as head of the Botanical Gardens at the University of British Columbia in 1968, the first opportunity presented itself. The Director, Dr. Alan Chan wanted to find a new Section Head with a PhD to replace Taylor. While he was looking for a suitable candidate, Chan needed someone to fill the position on an interim basis. My father had shared an office with Taylor for a number of years, and consequently was familiar with the job. Chan therefore asked him to take on this acting role until Dr. John McNeil, who would be coming over from England, could fill it. Unfortunately, McNeil did not last long in the position. Once again, Chan asked my father to take on the role of acting Section Head. At this point, staff began to lobby Chan to appoint my father permanently to the job. Staff had been happy with my father's leadership. They said, "He is doing the job, give it to him." So Chan did.

A big step on the road to becoming Director occurred in 1974, when the Director, Dr. Dave Hardwick, was informed that the job descriptions of all the technicians in the Institute were out-of-date. He was instructed to update them. He asked his Assistant Director, Dr. Don Oliver, to undertake this task. My father states, "Oliver, who was an entomologist, was not interested in botany whatsoever. He completed the revised job descriptions exclusively for the entomologists and submitted them." The person responsible for reviewing the classification submissions did a spot check of the information by meeting with some of the technicians. He discovered that a lot of the information was incorrect. He turned them all down. Hardwick was then faced with a situation where his superiors wanted this done and the person doing it was having difficulty. He asked my father, the Head of the Vascular Plant Section, if he would complete the job descriptions for all the technicians in botany and mycology. He agreed. "I went around and interviewed all the technicians and the scientists they reported to. I wrote up new job descriptions and checked everything thoroughly to make sure the information was accurate. I then submitted the information to Classifications. Once again a spot check was done. Everything was fine, so all the descriptions were accepted."

As part of his submission, my father had included a recommendation for a specific classification for each technician according to his or her job description. He says, "I provided an explanation for why each met the proposed classification criteria. For two of the job descriptions, I determined that the people were doing less than what was required for the level they were already classified under." He explained this to the head of Classifications. "I didn't do this to get these people demoted, I just wanted to have the assurance that these people would be red circled. This would be a flag for future reclassification exercises." In the meantime, my father planned to talk to the affected technicians and their supervising scientists to see if they could be assigned other tasks that would help justify their current classification. It also turned out that some of the technicians received reclassifications upward. Some even got reclassifications two grades higher.

When the technicians in entomology and zoology heard about this, of course, they immediately wanted similar treatment. Hardwick informed my father he had done such a good job, he wanted him to work with Oliver to do the same for entomology. My father declined, saying it was Oliver's job as Assistant Director to complete this task. "I had not minded doing the job for my colleagues in botany and mycology, but I didn't feel it was my duty to do it for entomology." Hardwick offered to make my father an Assistant Director. My father responded, "That's all well and good, but I'll only agree to do it if I do it by myself." Once again, my father found that there was no relationship between the job descriptions and what people were actually doing. He wrote new job descriptions and classified everyone accordingly, with some recommended for promotion. They were all accepted.

One of the people who had been red circled was a botanical technician. My father knew this person was a very good worker, but he was doing the same thing he had been doing for the last fifteen years. My father remembers interviewing him and being asked, "Other people got reclassifications upward, how come I didn't? Some of them aren't as good workers as I am." My father replied, "That's true, but it is what they are doing that makes the difference. They are working at a much higher level than you are. If you want to get a reclassification, you have to take on and learn new skills and do different work." The technician's response was, "Oh no, I like what I'm doing!" This straightforward, analytical approach would become the hallmark of my father's management style.

By 1978, when Hardwick wanted to take a one-year position at the University of California Berkeley, it had reached the stage where my father became the only person capable of taking over while he was away. Dr. Bill Mountain, the Director General at the time, was only willing to give his permission for Hardwick to leave if my father agreed to take over the position for the year. My father was interested in the assignment but hesitant because it would mean having to deal directly with the other Assistant Director, Don Oliver, and they did not get along. Hardwick was sufficiently motivated in his desire to go to Berkeley that he arranged for Oliver to step down as Assistant Director.

Within a week of Hardwick's return from California, he informed Mountain that he intended to retire. Mountain talked to Institute staff. They wanted my father confirmed permanently in the position. This was something my father had not anticipated. "I was quite happy doing research and had enjoyed dabbling in management in acting positions, but was reluctant to take on the role permanently." He says, "At that time there were significant problems in the Institute that I was not happy about, especially in entomology. I felt that if I tried to deal with the problems, I would make many enemies. I was not sure that I was willing to do that."

Mountain thought differently. "I want you to be my new Director. You are the best person for the job." He felt it was a natural progression for my father to become Director. "Mountain would have been vaguely aware of the problems in entomology, but I never told him that these problems were the main reason I was hesitant about accepting the position," my father says. Finally, Mountain came down on him hard about becoming the next Director, saying, "You have reached a stage where we have trained you, and I expect you to take on the job. If you don't take it, you will no longer be a Section Head, you will have no responsibility, and you will have to go back and spend the rest of your career looking through a microscope."

My father was actually surprised when Mountain was so strident in his desire that he become Director. It rather appealed to him, but he really had to think about accepting the position. If he took the job knowing about all the problems going on, he knew he was going to have stress-related health problems. "I came home and talked to Margaret. I said I really don't want to be

Director because there are all these things going on that I'm not happy with and if things continue on after I'm Director, I would be very unhappy. I just could not cope with such a situation." In the end, it was the encouragement of my mother, who thought he should go for it, that finally convinced my father to take on this new challenge.

Upon accepting the job as Director, my father decided to follow one simple rule. He would only do things that he personally thought were right and that he felt comfortable with. This way he would not have to come home and fret that he was doing something that he did not want to do, but something he was doing for a good reason. "Looking back, it was the best decision I ever made. I did not care what people thought, if I was comfortable with what I was doing. It gave me a great sense of freedom. It also allowed me to do things that people were often amazed at," he says. My father continued to use this approach when he became Acting Director General. "It certainly helped that my wife was one hundred percent in support of what I was doing and the possible consequences."

Compounding my father's worries about taking on the job was the fact that his main supporter, Bill Mountain, left Agriculture Canada soon after convincing him to become Director. Several years later, my father found out that Mountain had been involved in a power struggle with Dr. Ed LeRoux to become Assistant Deputy Minister of Agriculture Canada. Mountain lost.

- October 5, 1979 – Received a bombshell that Mountain will be seconded for a year. I will arrange an appointment with Mountain on Tuesday to tell him that I am not interested in being Director of BRI (the Biosystematics Research Institute).

- October 9, 1979 – I met with Mountain this morning and he just about ordered me to stay as Director.

- August 17, 1983 – Jake von Schaek filled me in on the

reasons that Mountain was ousted from Agriculture Canada.

Also instrumental to my father's comfort in taking on the role of Director was the decision to keep up with his research. "If worst came to worst, I could go back to being a research scientist," he says. Consequently, he continued to work consistently, if sporadically, on research during the entire time he was a manager. It drove the Assistant Deputy Minister, Ed LeRoux, crazy when he tried to summon my father to his office, that quite often my father's executive secretary would inform him, "Oh he's over in botany looking through the microscope." LeRoux hated to hear this. He would rant, "I told that guy he's a Director, not a scientist. I don't know what he's doing over there!" Carson confirms LeRoux's dislike of this situation by zealously stating, "Yes, yes, yes! He was critical of it. But, your father got his job done. He had no trouble doing both jobs. He was always in early. He would be in before me. He would get his management work done first and then go over to do some research. There was never anything not completed."

My father would just ignore LeRoux's comments. Doing research was part of my father's secret to coping with departmental intrigues. It enabled him to stand up fearlessly to the unreasonably demands of senior managers, because he always felt he could easily return to being a full-time researcher, and would have been quite happy to do so. He says, "I always kept up my research and even kept my technician. Whenever I had time, I had a little cubby hole over in the Saunders Building where I could go to work on my research. Initially, it was as a safety net in case I didn't like being a manager, but really it was also because I liked doing research." When asked if his fellow scientists admired his ability to take a strong stand with senior management, he agrees that they probably did. "Many of them would have benefitted from it," he says. "Keeping in touch with research also helped with my credibility when dealing with the other scientific staff."

⚘ April 20, 1978 – Went to Saunders Building in morning for

first time since Hardwick left. Spent whole morning in greenhouse scoring *Rorippa* crosses.

∅ April 4, 1979 – I spent afternoon over in Botany. I seem to be about finished with hard portion of Director's work. My experience since Jan. 1 leaves me with little respect for Hardwick who did little with 1 or 2 Assistant Directors to help him.

∅ October 17, 1979 – Spent first whole day in Saunders in ages. I started Biology of Weeds paper on *Cicuta*.

∅ March 25, 1981 – I spent the whole afternoon in botany identifying *Draba*. The first time in ages.

∅ November 19, 1981 – Finished Director General's job by 11 am and spent rest of day looking at chromosomes.

∅ May 12, 1982 – This is the first three days that I have spent mostly on research in the last seven months.

∅ January 12, 1984 – I received galley for *Rorippa sylvestris* paper today. Is this my last research paper?

One of the reasons that my father ended up as a manager was that he always liked to have six different things going on at the same time. He says, "I really liked to have a full day, with a lot of variability. As I've gotten older, I find it more difficult to handle several things at the same time." That said, he is still able to handle a heck of lot more than others his age.

Upon becoming Director, my father moved right away to address the problems in the Institute. He said to his executive secretary, Rosanna (Menchini) Carson, "It's a new ball game!" She knew what was going on, having also been a personal secretary to the previous Director. "We're going to do everything on the up and up. I might do things wrong, but they are going to be things I think are the right thing to do at the time. I am not going to do things that I know are absolutely wrong." He was also worried that eventually the problems would come to light. He was right. Five years after he became Director, the Institute was audited. If the problems had still occurred when the auditors came, they would have all been in big trouble. "It would have been a scandal," he says.

- March 15, 1984 – We had a chap in today to do an audit. He will be around for some time.

- April 4, 1984 – We received debriefing from the Auditor General and they have very few criticisms.

- June 13, 1985 – Met with management auditors at 11 am and they said that I was the most organized manager they had ever seen.

- December 17, 1985 – The auditors said that I should patent our activity statements.

- February 4, 1986 – Had a talk with the auditors today. They are going to suggest computerization of Operational Plans. They want more detail but do not realize how little my 'superiors' are interested in what we do.

- April 3, 1986 – Our gang listened to the auditor's report. We received almost a clean bill of health from them.

- April 7, 1986 – It looks as if we are going to get a terrific recommendation from the auditors.

Carson, who thoroughly enjoyed working with my father, concurs, "Things did change in the Institute once your father became Director. But he handled change very diplomatically." She remembers one incident when a technician was caught using the Agriculture Canada truck to go shopping. A member of the public saw her and reported it. Right away, your father called her in to address the problem. When she came out, she told me, "I understand what he's saying." There was no animosity.

Evert Linquist, the entomology Section Head during the time my father was Director, tells me, "In working with Gerry, what most remains in my mind was his tendency to go with his 'gut feeling' when we coped with difficult issues of management. In the midst of verbally presenting one's thoughts or sides on matters, one could often see at some point that his decision was made by the look of his eyes, almost as if little shades drew over them, and a slight negative movement of his head. Rightly or wrongly, these abbreviated deliberations and kept meetings in progress."

My father laughs when he hears Linquist's observation. He comments, "When I was Assistant Director to Hardwick, I would have to sit through Section Head meetings that would go on and on. These regular meetings would include representatives from ten different sections. Some of them would have their own little agendas. They would not be interested in the overall issues of the Institute; they were just performing to draw attention to themselves. Hardwick would let them take over meetings." When my father became Director, as soon as these individuals would start to take control of the meeting, he would shut them down. He made sure that they stayed focused on the business at hand. "This resulted in much shorter meetings and we actually arrived at decisions," he says. Part and parcel with this was that, one by one, he replaced problem section heads with people who were more positive and constructive to deal with.

My father's perception was that most of those at the meeting were so wrapped up in their own little universe that they didn't even notice what he was doing. He is not surprised that Linquist did. "More than most people, he was aware of what was going on," he says. As he thinks about it, my father comments, "At the point where my eyes started to glaze over, Linquist probably felt the same way most of the time. Even when Linquist disagreed with me on something, I always thought that he could see my point of view. That is certainly a lot more than I can say for many of the other scientists. A lot of them were only concerned with their own little areas of research." He pauses and then corrects himself, "They weren't even all that interested in their own research; they were only interested in promoting themselves. I always felt that Evert Linquist would have made a good Director." While he did function as Section Head, Linquist always steered away from getting any further involved in anything that would interfere with his research. His primary focus was always in advancing as an entomologist.

My father had many conflicts with his Assistant Deputy Minister, Dr. Ed LeRoux. LeRoux, a former entomologist, kept trying to interfere with the business of the Institute. He habitually tried to tell my father who he wanted promoted. If they didn't deserve the promotion, my father refused to support these demands. My father finally told him, "It's none of your business." My father's diaries document a number of instances where unhappy staff bypassed him and took their complaints directly to LeRoux. My father confirms this. They would try to get LeRoux to intervene. He comments, "Sometimes it worked, but most of the time it didn't. As soon as I found out what they were up to, I would call them on it. If they really insisted on bypassing me and LeRoux insisted on supporting them, I would document this in their next appraisal. I might say something along the lines of, they went to the Assistant Deputy Minister. I don't agree with his assessment of the situation. It is not borne out by their performance."

LeRoux never threatened my father directly, verbally or in writing. "He always did it through his executive assistant," my father says. His assistant would call and warn my father, "You know that Dr. LeRoux is not very happy with you. Maybe you should do such and such." When my father declined to take the advice, the assistant would respond with, "Well, that is probably going to affect your performance review. You are not going to get your performance bonus if you do that." In other words, if you want your bonus, you will do what Dr. LeRoux wants you to do. My father was always clear on telling the messenger that he was not going to play that game. While his approach to dealing with his superior managers did affect, to a certain extent, the bonuses my father received during his career as a manager, it did not cause him to alter his methods.

One person LeRoux wanted promoted was not even doing what he was hired to do. My father had rated this person as unsatisfactory. LeRoux wanted him promoted to Research Scientist 4. In my father's opinion, he didn't even deserve to be a Research Scientist 3. My father was certainly not going to recommend him for reclassification. The Acting Director General at the time, Ron Halstead, warned my father, "You can't do that! Ed's not going to like it. Ed told me that he expects you to recommend this guy for promotion." In spite of this warning, my father still refused to endorse the person. LeRoux, through Halstead, tried to get my father to change his recommendation. My father stated, "He can't change it. There is a place for his recommendation and a place for mine. He can't change mine. It's illegal. He can put down on the form that he thinks this guy is a super scientist. He can then forward it to the Committee for a decision. But he has to leave mine." All reclassifications at the senior scientist level are handled by a national inter-departmental committee. LeRoux continued to persist in his attempts to intimidate my father into changing his recommendation. Finally, my father told Halstead "If LeRoux doesn't back off, I'm prepared to take out a formal grievance against him." Halstead was shocked and repeated his mantra, "You can't do that!" But my father was determined. With my father's track record, Halstead decided to try talking to LeRoux. Halstead finally came back and said, "Ed has decided to make a compromise. He will retype the form and he will leave your recommendation blank, with just his recommendation." Halstead asked, "What do you think of that?" My father responded, "I intend to formally start my grievance against him." This was followed by a telephone call from LeRoux's executive secretary. "Ed's very angry with you. It's not going to do your career any good. That said, we are going to leave your recommendation in place and Dr. LeRoux will add his recommendation. It will go forward to the Committee like that."

Well, time went by. My father was finally notified that the

submission had been turned down. Sometime later, my father was talking with Chuck Gruchy, who worked at the National Museum. Gruchy was the Museum's representative on the inter-departmental committee panel. My father couldn't help asking, "What did people say when this submission came up?" Gruchy gleefully responded, "Oh it was interesting! Do you know who was representing Environment Canada on the panel? Bill Mountain." Mountain was now Assistant Deputy Minister at Environment Canada, the same Bill Mountain who was responsible for my father becoming Director. When Mountain came across the submission he apparently said, "Look at this! I know this scientist (the subject of the reclassification). He was a terrible scientist. I had nothing but trouble with him. Here, Ed LeRoux is recommending him and Mulligan, who is a good scientist and an honest guy, is not. If anyone around this table is going to support this reclassification, we are going to be here all day!" They immediately all responded simultaneously "Turned down!"

After the reclassification fiasco, my father was not one of LeRoux's favoured employees, to say the least. This never bothered my father at all. Nothing is more aggravating than someone who can't be manipulated. In an ironic twist, even though my father's strong ethics caused senior managers a lot of aggravation, he was always first on their list to replace them when they were away. The position of Director General involved making decisions about a lot of money and resources. My father was one of the few people a succession of Director Generals trusted to act in the position, sometimes for many months.

My father is a fighter; he doesn't give up easily: "If I feel strongly about something, I will stick my neck out in stating my case," he says. His executive secretary, Carson, makes a similar comment: "He stuck to his beliefs. You weren't going to budge him. He was stubborn. But he cared." In retrospect, my father comments, "Most of the time the results have been favourable, but a few times this approach caused me problems." This tussle with LeRoux is a good example of his perseverance in the face of great opposition, obtaining a favourable result, but also causing him many problems with senior managers. He was viewed among senior managers as not playing the game — well their game anyway.

At work, he developed this ethical approach quite early, because he found that without it, he would get stomach pains doing something with which he was not comfortable. He is hesitant to credit his strong ethics to his Catholic upbringing because he knows many Catholics who clearly don't exhibit an ethical approach to how they conduct themselves. The person he does credit for his outlook on life is his mother. She had very strong ethics based both on her devout Catholic beliefs and on the person she intrinsically was. My father also believes that he inherited his ability to make decisions from her.

Interestingly, in my father's opinion, one of the most ethical people in the Institute was Clarie Frankton, an atheist. As my father grew older, he found that there was no correlation between being religious and being good. "Some people think that church-going, god-fearing people are wonderful people. But I have found that a good number are not. Some of the worst and most immoral people I have known attend church regularly. They justify everything by the fact that they are churchgoers. I feel that a lot of the problems in the world are due to religion, one religion against another," he says.

My father firmly believes that it is a very rare senior manager who is not corrupt to some degree. The reality is that to reach the top levels of management, terrible compromises are difficult to avoid. Even with his strong moral code, my father includes himself in this category. For instance, in mid-November 1981, when he took over as Acting Director General for six months, he discovered some interesting information. My father is a friendly guy. During this time, he got to know a lot of the

Director General's staff quite well, the clerks and, in particular, all the financial staff. One day, he was sitting around talking to the financial staff when he asked about why he never received an annual increase to his budget, while other Directors did. "How come I never get these increases, when so and so, who is a terrible manager gets a big increase every year?" One of them said, "Gerry, the problem is, you always manage your Institute well. You always manage your budget. These other Directors are always in the hole, so we have to bail them out." My father was amazed, "What do you mean you bail them out? Where do you get the money?" He was told, "At the end of every year, there are usually big projects that aren't completed. For instance, this year, we were going to build an addition onto the lab in Lethbridge. We were not able to do it, so we still have this money. If we don't use the money, we will lose it." He responded, "What do you mean, you will lose it?" The response was, "We can't carry it over to the next year. So we look at these other Directors who are always over budget and we give them extra money." Out of curiosity, my father asked, "What would happen if I said I need another three-quarters of a million dollars?" They told him, "Just say you are going to go in the hole by that amount." My father was incredulous, "You mean that's all I have to do?"

My father immediately went to talk to his institute's administrative officer, Andre Giroux and declared, "New budget! We just got three-quarters of a million dollars to spend." Giroux responded excitedly, "Oh! Where did you get it?" My father replied, "Don't ask!" So they budgeted carefully for this overrun. As he had been told, he was forgiven for it at the end of the year, and the next year he got more. So he started to play the game. He told himself he was doing it for his staff and the work of the Institute. But he felt that he had compromised his values in doing so.

✍ October 20, 1981 – Heard today that we were not going to get any more money this year. As I manage this way, I don't see any change from usual. It certainly will affect those that go $90,000 in the hole and expect others to pick up the money deficit.

⊠ February 3, 1983 – I heard that they are going to pick up all my overspending of O&M (Operation and Maintenance) and that I will get an extra $25K.

In a similar vein, the first Branch Management Committee of Director Generals of each of the regions in Canada that my father attended was a real eye-opener for him. During the meeting, they would discuss policy issues. They would have back-and-forth discussions until they arrived at a reasonable decision. At the end of the meeting, the Assistant Deputy Minister who chaired the meeting would say, "Okay, so now, how are we going to announce these new policy decisions to staff?" Communication staff at the meeting would recommend, "You should say this..." My father would sit there listening incredulously, thinking, "That's not what we decided! That's not the reason we decided to do that!" It turned out the reasons they announced bore no resemblance to the discussion at the meeting. He found out in the next six months that they did this all the time.

More and more, my father discovered that all the managers at that level did things like this. "They don't tell you the truth. It's not what happened, it's what they want you to think happened." Since that time, he never believes anything that senior managers or politicians say. "There is the reason given and then there is the real reason. They are doing it to help themselves climb the management ladder, to get votes, or as a favour to someone else," he says.

Several times my father was Acting Director General of the Central Experimental Farm. He knows perfectly well that if he had been made permanent in the position, he would have ended up doing the same thing. Little by little, you say to yourself, "Well, that's what you've got to do to survive." This was one of the things that led to his decision to retire. He realized he was going to be drawn into things he didn't think were right if he continued to work at that level. He decided that he didn't want to have anything to do with it. He made the decision to "go back to the bench" as he puts it, to being a scientist. To concentrate on doing the work he loved best.

In the end, the key to my father's success as a manager was that he never wanted to be a manager at all costs. As a result, he was able to take chances and to push the envelope much more than those who did. He also got a lot of personal satisfaction from simply doing a good job. He credits this approach for how he advanced in Agriculture Canada far beyond what someone would expect with his education. He did many things for personal satisfaction and did them without any thought of reward. Most of the promotions he received, he got because someone else who was supposed to be doing the job, wasn't and consequently they would be looking around for someone who would. He usually took on the job as a challenge and because he got satisfaction from doing it. Once he was doing the job for a while, they would finally give up on the person not doing the job and would say, "Well, why don't you do it?" Invariably he did.

13
ANNUAL UPSET

My father's diaries are full of upheaval and dramatics following the results of the yearly performance appraisals. Outrage and attempts to manipulate the situation were the order of the day. Many of the staff seemed to be always upset, no matter what the results of their appraisal. Nothing was ever good enough. I asked Rosanna (Menchini) Carson, his executive secretary, about all the upset. "Yes," she pipes up, "including me!"

The yearly performance appraisals were not something that my father looked forward to doing. His worst experience doing appraisals occurred the year that he was Acting Director. Dave Hardwick took off for Berkley, California, for a year, but let it be known that he wanted certain people recommended for advancement. The problem for my father was that most of these recommendations were not supported by the performance of the people involved. He was shocked to find out that many of the scientists weren't working on the things they had documented they were doing.

> ✍ April 11, 1978 – There are lots of proposals for reclassification (as part of annual assessment). Many of them are absurd.

Because Hardwick was still the Director, and my father was just acting in the position, he felt that he had to go along with what Hardwick wanted. However, he states, "I was not happy about the situation." In typically style, my father did push the envelope on a few things, as much as he felt he could. Once he became the permanent Director, the envelope really got pushed.

As the new Director, my father made sure that everything the scientists were doing was consistent with what they had stated they were doing. Soon after he became Director, one of the scientists came to see him. He told my father that Dr. Hardwick had put him in for a reclassification to Research Scientist 3, but that it had not gone through. He informed my father that this reclassification had been strongly recommended by Hardwick. He expected my father to do the same again at the next opportunity. My father replied that he would look into it. He asked Carson to retrieve a copy of Hardwick's submission. He then asked her to go over each of the publications listed on the submission to check their validity. At that time, a copy of all published papers was kept by the Director's office. Carson found that there was no evidence of most of the publications listed. My father went to see the scientist to ask him to explain. The scientist told him, "Well, I didn't publish them, but they are well advanced." He had been getting credit for work he had not published. This became my father's typical approach to finding the truth. He would go to the scientist and say, "Let me see it."

In fact, my father considers his management strategy for annual performance appraisals one of the most significant contributions he made during his tenure as Director of the Biosystematics Research Institute. A central part of his strategy was to interview staff members to find out what they were hired for and what research they were supposed to be doing. He did this every year. "I believe that the detailed documentation of accurate, up-to-date job descriptions resulted in everyone knowing exactly what they were supposed to be doing. I always made it clear to staff, especially the scientists, that this was just a guide. I told them that if they ever came up with anything important scientifically and it was not covered in the job description, that they should feel free to come and see me. The job description was always open for change."

"I always used to really enjoy visiting the scientists in their labs and asking them what they were doing, what the technician was doing, one-on-one. I was sincerely interested. There are many smart people in the Institute. I learned a lot from them. Being Director provides a wonderful overview of all the scientific disciplines. More than anything, this is what the staff really miss today," my father comments. He hears this all the time. "No one cares. They don't know what I'm doing. They have no interest in what I'm doing. I don't even know who my boss is anymore." My father laments, "It is a very sad state of affairs." It is also not conducive to productivity. In my father's experience as Director, a certain number of scientists are self-contained and self-motivated, but only about ten or fifteen percent of them, which means that the other eighty-five percent are drifting. "They don't know what they are doing. They are lost. For fifteen percent of the people, it doesn't matter what you do, they are going to produce and be good employees."

My father always had the philosophy that if a person didn't meet the objectives of the job despite having tried hard, but weren't capable of meeting them, he was always lenient. Instead, he would work with them to suggest that they change their project and take on something easier for them. But, if somebody didn't reach the objectives because they were lazy or because they cheated, he was merciless. He would come down on them hard. "I found that most of the staff were quite happy with this approach, because they knew exactly where they stood. People who were borderline would often smarten up, to their own benefit," he says.

In my father's world, appraisals were a reflection of effort. "I took the annual appraisals seriously. I tried to rate people to the best of my abilities, which in some cases meant some people weren't very happy." Many people who had never been given credit for their work were duly recognized, while those who had been given disproportionate credit for their efforts, no longer were. "Lots of people were really upset by this new regime, while others were delighted," he says. In general, he found that the good scientists were very happy with him as Director. It was the poor scientists, the people who had been slacking, who were not happy with him.

Part and parcel with the job descriptions was the requirement that everything had a deadline. "No task was to go on forever," he strongly states. My father would ask scientists to estimate how long it would take to complete their research. If they said three years, my father would say, "Fine, it has to be done in that timeframe." This schedule was reviewed annually. "If it was not going to be done, I wanted to know why. If you had a good reason for delays, the timing could be adjusted accordingly. After all, I was a scientist. I know things happen," he says. However, if they didn't have a good reason, he was equally aware of when people weren't doing what they should have been doing.

"Before I became Director, a lot of the scientists had projects that went on and on forever, with no accountability whatsoever. Some of them worked on the same project for their whole career. Others would start one project, lose interest, and then start another, only to lose interest again. This resulted in multiple incomplete research projects. The very good scientists were very focused and organized, producing consistently and efficiently. Once I became Director, every project had to be approved by me," my father states.

"As a taxonomist, I was knowledgeable about how long things should last. The scientists had to convince me of what they wanted to do and that it would result in some sort of product, such as a monograph or treatment. Some research projects could be quite short, a year, while others could take five years. It was rare for a project to last longer than five years. Every project was also reviewed every year. For some scientists it was traumatic. Some weren't producing and in some cases there was no record of whether anything had ever been published," my father says. Seeing poor producers being held to account boosted staff morale. Seeing those who performed well given due credit had the same result. It brought fairness to the Institute.

"When people were not pulling their weight, I would rate them as unsatisfactory at performance reviews. In the second year I was Director, I had five research scientists that I rated as unsatisfactory. At the national committee that reviewed appraisals, I found out that in all of Canada that year there were only five scientists rated unsatisfactory, all of them by me," he says. My father found this to be a very effective management technique in many ways. "Because I was honest in my assessment of my staff, when I appeared at the national committee to decide who would get promotions, when I rated someone highly, the committee would always approve the promotion," he comments.

⌖ January 14, 1980 – Received all assessments for central region today and went over them. It appears that most of the Directors are very lenient with poor producers.

⌖ January 16, 1981 – Received Institute appraisals and it is obvious that other Directors did not rate their staff very objectively.

"Most of the scientists were very hard-working people, but a certain percentage felt that once they obtained their PhD they could just coast the rest of the way. I felt that about twenty-five percent of the scientists didn't deserve the positions and salaries they were already getting. Some of them were incredibly arrogant," my father says. As Director, he made a point of consistently calling these people to account for their poor performance and behaviour. He says, "I hit them right between the eyes with a sledgehammer. Once they knew they couldn't coast anymore, many of these people left to work somewhere else or retired." Either solution was fine with him. They became someone else's problem. "I just didn't have any patience with staff who were not pulling their weight," he says. In contrast, he always had great sympathy for anyone who, for one reason or another, was struggling with what they were working on, but were obviously trying hard. For these people, he was more than happy to go out of his way to try to help them. But, "I had no time for overqualified and arrogant people who spent all their time causing problems for other people," he firmly states.

"After a year or so, I found fewer and fewer people complained about their appraisals. They may have whined behind my back, but they didn't do it to my face. It would also have become obvious to them that whining had a very negative effect on me. If they complained about their performance rating, my response was, well fine, we'll sit down and go over the specifications of what is required for a research scientist at your level. We will review your productivity and performance as compared to the specifications," he says. My father was always willing to meet with any of his staff to discuss their performance. He found that it quickly became obvious that few really wanted to take him up on his offer. Often, such a review revealed that he had actually been a little lenient in his evaluation relative to the actual job requirements. My father was known to say, "Well actually, if you go by the specifications, you really shouldn't be at the level you are as it is."

My father agrees that the pressure to publish, a key factor in scientific performance reviews, has a big influence on the behaviour of scientists. "I never thought that the specifications for publication were fair. I always felt that the emphasis placed on publications in the research branch of Agriculture Canada should not be as strict as it is. There were staff that were not top scientists but were valuable to Agriculture Canada and particularly the Canadian taxpayer because they produced a lot of very useful and more applied information. Then there were scientists who did nothing for the Canadian taxpayer, but could crank out very sophisticated papers. These were the people that were rewarded by the system and advanced through the ranks," he says. As a manager, my father was constantly frustrated because there was no way for him to reward those who produced useful information. He tried hard to get the job specifications changed to give more recognition to people who were producing things that were of some importance to the Canadian taxpayer. He was never successful in doing this. It was an ongoing source of frustration for him.

My father always felt that his executive secretary, Rosanna (Menchini) Carson, did more than she was paid to do. She kept an up-to-date list of everyone's research papers on file. This allowed my father to know what was going on with all the scientists and technicians. Carson was instrumental in his ability to do this. My father says, "To a degree, tracking of the scientists was initiated by Dr. Hardwick. However, the flaw in Hardwick's approach was that he just took the word of people about what they said they were doing. He never followed up to verify the information." With Carson's help, he did. My father says, "I relied on her a lot. She was good at keeping track of everything. If I had had a poor secretary, I would have had a lot of trouble."

Carson told me that the next Director, Robert Trottier, thought she was too emotional. When I mention this to my father, he stops, thinks about it, and says, "Rosanna was an emotional person, but I wouldn't say she was too emotional. She was sensitive. She could easily take offence to something, especially to one of the scientists who were very sure of themselves. Often, good scientists don't care what they have to do to get what they want. It is a justifiable means to an end. If she didn't understand this, they could be very rough on her. The fact that I was a scientist and understood where they were coming from, I never took what they did personally. I always got along very well with scientists who cared about what they were doing."

Another key tool in my father's evaluation of scientists was citation abstracts. An international organization goes through all the scientific papers each year and lists the number of references by author. This information is summarized in a publication called *Citation Abstracts*. My father found it a very useful publication and he used it extensively. "If a research scientist claimed that he or she was tops in their field, I could consult the publication and find out for the last five years, how often they were cited by other authors. There were two factors that I considered. First, if other scientists quoted the Institute scientist in their papers, it showed the number of times they were cited in a given year. But you also had to know something about the individual's work because in some cases, they were cited because their research was so poor they were being lambasted in the literature. So the number of citations is only an indication. If someone was rarely quoted, it also said something about the value of his or her research. People were either ignoring them or didn't think enough of the importance of their research to cite them."

When my father thinks back, he feels it was a big advantage to him as a manager that he had been through the ranks, from fieldworker to technician and on up the line. He always got along with the support staff and a big part of that was probably because he had been there and a lot of them realized that and appreciated it. "Some people when they move up, shit on the guys below them, but I always felt for them," he says. He never forgot to put himself in their place. Dan Brunton, a local field naturalist with many friends at the Farm, sees this from another perspective, "Your father went from being one of the guys to being the boss. That's a tough transition for many working relationships to make without damage, especially in a place like the Farm where the politics are so complex."

Stephen Darbyshire, a biologist in the Institute, adds yet another perspective. "He was not liked by everyone. He did not tolerate shadiness or incompetence. Those who had benefited through sloppy behaviour or favouritism, tended to dislike him. Those who appreciated fairness and worked closely with him tended to like him. Those who were fair, conscientious, and worked hard got your father's respect." Darbyshire also stated, "Unpopular decisions had to be made and your father did not have problems making decisions. Many appreciated him as someone who understood their craft, their needs, and their place in the Institute."

Carson gives me her point-of-view, "Mr. M expected staff to get their jobs done. Yes, he could be firm when he needed to be. If you were doing your job, you were treated with respect. If you were not, you heard about it." My father is not surprised to hear Carson's comments. "If there was something that I felt was wrong and had to be addressed, I did it. Frankly, if I didn't do it, I'd be sick about it. It would bother me if something was going on and I felt I had the power to deal with it and I wasn't doing so. It may have seemed as if I was being strict, but it was just me dealing with things to protect my mental health."

According to Stephen Darbyshire, since my father's retirement, they have not had a Director who clearly understood the scientists' work. No one has risen through the ranks. Now they tend to parachute people in, with the philosophy that a manager can manage anything. Even those who were not fans of my father now often long for the days when he was Director.

Only recently, Paul Catling introduced my father as the former Director to a new scientist hired by the Institute. In doing so, Catling commented, "Everyone was afraid of him. He was a tough Director. People didn't want to cross him." My father was surprised by these comments. He reflects on this and then says, "Both Paul Catling and Evert Linquist have told me that I was by far the best Director they ever had because everyone always knew where they stood with me. Since I retired, they have never known where they stand with managers." Catling further elaborates, "You don't know what you're supposed to be doing. With you, we did. If we were doing the right thing, then you knew you were fine. If not, we knew you were unhappy and you told us so."

"The person who knows a lot about what went on in the Institute was Rosanna," my father says. Carson had been the personal secretary of Dr. Hardwick when he was Director, then she was my father's personal secretary the entire time he was Director. She had the same position with Robert Trottier for a few years after my father retired. My father comments, "Everything that went on, she knew about it. On certain things, she probably knew more than I did, because people were likely more up-front with her in expressing their feelings than they would have been to me." When my father remembers how people dealt with him, he is not so naïve that he doesn't know that they put a better face on when they talked to him. They would not have said things to him that they would have said behind his back. Some people hung on his every word when he was Director, as they would have for anyone in that position.

When I talked to Carson, I mention that my father always figured that staff might have presented a different face about their feelings to others than they did directly to him. Carson is quick to say, "No, I very rarely heard negative things about your Dad from the scientists." She says, "There was not a lot of negativity during his time as Director. The only thing that the scientists resented was his not having a PhD, yet was able to become Director. That was the extent of it. If they had had any complaints, they certainly realized after he retired that they had lost a great man." There was greater appreciation of him in hindsight.

14
ENTOMOLOGY

My father's diaries are rife with entries about his frustration with entomologists and the amount of management time he had to devout to them compared to staff in other sections of the Biosystematics Research Institute.

- January 31, 1978 – I have spent about 90% of my time on entomology problems since Dave Hardwick left.

- June 29, 1979 – I seem to spend a greater proportion of my time servicing entomology, certainly out of proportion with the number of staff.

- March 23, 1984 – Work is beginning to get me down. I feel further and further away from plant staff, but not very close to zoologists or others.

Since my father is a botanist, I wondered if this was a clash of disciplines or whether there was more to the story. My father is surprised by the question. He thinks about it and says, "Part of it was that there are a lot more entomologists than any other discipline in the Institute. This is because there are far more insects in Canada, and indeed the world, compared to plants. Even in beetles, there are probably more types in Canada than all the vascular plants in Canada. Entomologists often deal with many, many organisms, but their main goal is to put names to all of them. For botanists, there are fewer plants, so they are able to get to know them better. As a result, botanists become more interested in what these plants are associated with in their habitats."

My father goes on to say, "Most of the entomologists in the Institute were good to deal with. However, a few people just exploited everything. Others exploited opportunities provided by these corrupting influences. Some people knew what was going on, but they just decided not to do anything about it." When my father became Director, he was told that a certain entomologist was untouchable. He knew people in high places and he was "untouchable." In my father's opinion, "The main reason that most of my management problems were in entomology was because that section let things go on a lot longer and further without dealing with them than other sections. The problems piled up and became entrenched. The previous Director, Dr. Hardwick, was a good scientist, but a weak manager. He didn't face up to anything. He always took the easy way out."

When my father was Acting Director, he found out that Mr. Untouchable had borrowed many insect specimens from various collections around the world, keeping them for a long time. My father found letters addressed to the previous Director from these institutions asking for their specimens to be returned. This situation wasn't being dealt with. As Acting Director, there was nothing my father could do about it. However, once my father became Director, one of the first things he did was to take steps to rectify the problem. He called in Jack Martin, who was considered the head technician in entomology. Martin was supposed to be in charge of the insect collection. However, my father soon found out that Martin wasn't in charge at all, and was not considered by the entomologists to have any authority over the collection. My father gave Martin the authority. He told Martin that his first assignment was to find out what had happened to all the specimens that people were asking to be returned. Martin was horrified, "I can't go into his office!" My father responded, "That's your job. That's what you were hired for. That's your classification. You get down there and look." So, Martin did. He reported back the disturbing information that many of the specimens didn't exist anymore. My father says, "Mr. Untouchable hadn't put them away into storage cabinets. They were lying around his office and live bugs had eaten the dead insects right off the pins. So all this typed insect material borrowed from other institutions was gone."

My father then called this entomologist in and asked, "What's going on?" He demanded that he prepare a list of all the specimens that were gone or damaged. My father then used this information to write the affected institutions and tell them what the status of their specimens was and to apologize for the condition of them. My father also told Mr. Untouchable that from then on, he would not be allowed to borrow any more specimens, from anyone. This was a terrible embarrassment for the Institute. My father eventually found out that many of the other institutions knew what was going on and had become resigned to the fact that they were never going to get their specimens back. Some of the institutions would not allow anyone from Agriculture Canada to borrow specimen material from them anymore. My father felt that if the Institute owned up to what had happened and put their house in order, that he could re-establish these damaged relationships.

Once the problem came to light, my father found out that other Institute entomologists with offices near Mr. Untouchable's were terrified that the damage to specimens would spread to their collections. "I was shocked. This was the National entomology collection! Its care and storage was a disgrace," he says with disgust. In order to make sure this would never happen again, my father identified a good, responsible entomologist from each of the eight entomological units to act as a curator representing their section. In doing so, he was careful to select individuals who valued the collection. He called them all to a meeting and told them he was going to establish a curatorial committee, with a designated head curator.

My father also used this committee to deal with another problem, the inappropriate issuance of tax receipts to entomologists. Some of the entomologists were collecting insects, supposedly on their vacations. They were having other scientists put a monetary value on the specimens and then donating them to the National Collection in exchange for income tax receipts, sometimes worth thousands of dollars. There were also cases where some university professors receiving grants from the National Research Council, a federal government agency, were donating some of their specimens in exchange for big income tax receipts. These professors also tended to be the ones evaluating material for some of the Agriculture Canada scientists.

Once again, my father had been aware of this practice while he was Acting Director, but felt unable to stop it. Once he became Director, he was determined to end it. In doing so, he set it up that anyone who wished to donate specimens to the National Insect Collection had to do so through the eight member curatorial committee. This committee would then be responsible for making an evaluation of whether the donated specimens would be worthwhile additions to the National Collection. If so, they would determine how much the donation was worth. All of this had to be documented in a short report and sent to the Director, who would then decide whether an income tax receipt should be issued. Only then would my father agree to issue an income tax receipt.

⚬ November 21, 1980 – Gruchy told me today what the National Museum's policy is on income tax receipts for staff and research associates and adding to personal collections are forbidden at Museum.

- ✍ March 17, 1983 – I appeared before the Zoology curatorial committee regarding income tax receipts and they agreed with my proposal.

- ✍ March 16, 1984 – I sent guidelines for the collections to the Chairpersons of the Curatorial Committees.

Yet another entomological problem involved a special deal with the Entomology Society of Canada. My father describes the situation, "The deal was that papers submitted by Agriculture Canada entomologists would be charged page charges to the Society considerably higher than the fees they charged to everyone else. A large paper could cost the Department a lot of money. It was also arranged that the Agriculture Canada entomologists would receive reprints of their papers with fancy covers on them. The Society charged Agriculture Canada for these premium covers. As a result, the Society was making a lot of money through these various transactions. Essentially, the entomologists were trying to support their professional association with public funds. While this made them look good in the eyes of their fellow entomologists, it was being done wholly at the taxpayers' expense."

My father had some inkling of all these deals when he was Assistant Director, but when he became Acting Director he found out exactly what was going on. At first, he was shocked; he had not anticipated the extent of the problems. His knowledge of these unsavoury activities was one of the major reasons my father initially did not want to take on the job of Director of the Institute.

All that being said, it is important to note that not everything was negative in my father's relationship with the entomologists. At the time my father became Director, the entomologists were working on a manual of Arctic *diptera*. "*Diptera* are flies, all sorts of flies. It is a big order, and as such, it was a big and costly project to prepare this manual. Entomologists from all around the world contributed material to the manual, but it was headed up by Agriculture Canada. One of the entomologists was in charge of the manual, but under his leadership, the project was going on and on and on, with no end in sight," says my father. When he became Director, my father stated, "That's enough!"

To bring it to a head, my father called together all the *diptera* scientists to discuss the situation. It turned out that they were all unhappy with what was going on. He informed them that he wanted someone else to take over the project. My father put Frank McAlpine in charge, with Monty Wood to assist him. He then put pressure on the two of them to get the work done. The problem was that one of the Institute entomologists was supposed to produce a particular section for the manual. Everyone else had submitted his or her sections, but this one contribution was still not finished. The entomologists were worried. "What are we going to do? We can't do without his section." My father finally declared, "Forget about him. He will not be included." So it was published without it. Although it never occurred to my father at the time, years later it really irritated him that his important contribution in getting the *diptera* scientists organized and motivated was never acknowledged. The *Diptera Manual*, published in two parts, would never have been produced if it weren't for his persistence.

15
INSTITUTE ADVOCATE

During the time my father was Director of the Biosystematics Research Institute, located at the Central Experimental Farm in Ottawa, there were about one hundred and twenty employees in the Institute, half of them scientists and the other half technicians. Ninety percent of the staff was located in the Neatby Building on Carling Avenue, where my father also had his office. Only the botanical staff was housed in the more centrally located, historic, Saunders Building.

The Biosystematics Research Institute is involved in taxonomy. This means that botanists, mycologists, nematologists, bacteriologists, arachnologists, and entomologists work on the classification of their respective organisms and, to a certain extent, their biology. When an unknown species in any of these fields is found anywhere in Canada, the Biosystematics Research Institute in Ottawa is the first responder. When there is a sudden, unknown problem, the Institute would always have somebody who either was involved in research on the organism, was knowledgeable about the organism, or knew where to find the experts. As an example, my father says, "If a new insect was attacking a certain type of tree in British Columbia, the Institute entomologists would be called in. There are provincial entomologists, but they are typically specialists working on known pests for which they are trying to find controls. When something arises that they have never seen before, the first thing they would do is send a specimen to the Institute in Ottawa. The Institute has an identification service. If it were a beetle, it would go to the beetle experts. Even if they had never seen that particular beetle in Canada, they would know what zoological group it belonged in and would know if there were an expert working on that group at the United States Department of Agriculture, or somewhere in Europe or Russia. They would be able to get in touch with the right person quickly. Usually within a day or two they would know what the organism was, whether it was causing problems elsewhere, if there was cause for concern in Canada, and, if so, whether something needed to be set up to deal with it. After that, if it were localized, the province would put together a team that would be briefed by the Institute's experts. Following this, the province would take over and the federal staff would have nothing more to do with the situation. The Institute has dealt with many, many cases like this."

⌀ October 25, 1976 – John Slykies dropped around and asked me for help in discovering the cause of little cherry disease in the Okanogan Valley.[4] I told him that we would help and for him to write and outline his needs.

The Biosystematics Research Institute is also involved in international agricultural situations. My father recounts a case where a country in South America banned potatoes grown in the Canadian Maritime Provinces. "They claimed there was a pest in the potatoes. It turned out to be a purely political manoeuvre. This country was also growing potatoes and they were playing games in an effort to gain an economic advantage. Fortunately, in many cases the Institute staff are world

---

[4] John Slykies was a virologist with Agriculture Canada, stationed at the Okanogan Research Station. Little Cherry Disease is a virus carried by insects. It was affecting Bing cherries. He was looking for help from the Institute entomologists.

authorities, so when Agriculture Canada sent an expert in the field down to talk to their entomologists, they backed off because the Canadian scientists knew more about the situation. The core expertise was typically in Ottawa, but sometimes there would also be specialists on certain groups of organisms at Canadian universities. One such specialist in beetles was Dr. George Ball, a professor at the University of Alberta, in Edmonton. In certain areas, Ball would sometimes know more than the Institute beetle experts. He also often had students come to the Institute in Ottawa to work on beetles. Some of the Institute staff had also once been students studying under George Ball."

My father was proud of the knowledge and work of the Institute staff. He used to love dropping into offices in both buildings, asking, "How are things going? What are you doing? What have you found new? Show me?" He was equally interested in what the technicians were doing. When he heard something interesting, he wouldn't hesitate to commend them. "That sounds good. Good for you!" He really enjoyed this interaction.

This familiarity and interest had a side effect that was not always welcomed by my father. People always felt his office door was open. Typically, a steady stream of people wanted to come in and talk over their problems with him. While it was difficult at times, he always felt that it was part of his job to take on this role. Consequently, he got into the habit of arriving at the office early each day, between seven and seven-fifteen in the morning. Most of the staff that came to see him rarely did so until after nine o'clock. This would allow him to have two hours of uninterrupted time in which to concentrate on his management tasks.

His executive secretary, Carson, heartily agrees, "Without a doubt, your father had an open door policy, and when I say open door, I mean the door was always opened. Nothing was done in secret, unless it really was confidential. Staff could always rely on him. He was always available. Staff felt that they had someone to protect their interests. I really believe that was the general consensus among staff." This is echoed by Evert Linquist, an Institute entomologist, "I valued and respected the sincerity of your father's commitment to the direction and welfare of our Institute under circumstances from higher levels of management that were unpredictable and often trying."

When it came to getting resources that benefitted his Institute, my father did very well. He states, "I was successful because I prepared well-documented requests, because I was insistent, and ultimately because Ed LeRoux knew that if he didn't give me the resources I requested that I would make his life miserable. If it came down to a choice between me or another Director who did whatever LeRoux wanted them to do, he would give it to me." While this approach did not benefit my father personally, it certainly benefited the Institute. His diary documents very well the effort and anxiety my father endured in fighting for the Institute's interests.

- November 25, 1983 – I did not sleep well last night worrying about low support of biosystematics by those above me.

- February 1, 1985 – I represented Halstead, as acting Director General, at the BMC (Branch Management Committee) meeting. (Those designated to) defend the Research Branch position with the Neilson Committee are a poor bunch of wimps.

- October 4, 1985 – Halstead met with us and is proposing a 15 out of 35 reduction for BRI (Biosystematics Research Institute). I have decided to resign as Director, effective as soon as possible and will write a memo to Halstead on Monday. I actually drafted it today. I hope to go back to the bench.

- October 5, 1985 – (Sat.) I did not sleep well last night and finally got up and drafted a letter of resignation to Halstead. (Later in day) Came home and redrafted my letter. (That night) I decided not to give my letter to Halstead tomorrow. I will see how the land lies for the next little while.

⌀ October 7, 1985 – I wrote a stinky letter to Halstead regarding his treatment of BRI with a copy to LeRoux. I also wrote a letter to staff requesting suggestions for a new home for BRI, with a copy to Halstead.

⌀ October 8, 1985 – My caustic letters to Halstead and LeRoux paid off. Our person year reduction has been reduced from 15 to 1. Our staff may know nothing about it but I am on cloud nine.

⌀ October 17, 1985 – I heard that there will be a lot of layoffs and that several other Directors "donated" many blue collared workers and others to LeRoux. I am apparently narrow minded for fighting for my staff.

One of the most significant resources my father was able to acquire for the Institute was funding for steel cabinets to house the National Collection of insects and arachnids. The storage for entomological specimens had long been a problem. The quality of the cases was very poor and, in my father's opinion, the storage conditions for the National entomology collection had been a disgrace. Obtaining new entomological storage cases wasn't easy to do. In the early 1980s, no manufacturer in Canada produced the type of cases required to house all the specimens. My father comments, "To buy them at that time from the United States, when the Canadian dollar was only worth about sixty cents was not an option for us. We only had so much money to work with, and we simply couldn't afford it."

Their problem was finally resolved with help from the Smithsonian Institute in Washington. My father tells the story, "Every second year a group of entomologists and botanists from the Central Experimental Farm would visit the Smithsonian, and every other year, the Smithsonian's scientists would visit the Farm." Because of these frequent interactions, the scientists on both sides of the border got to know each other very well. He goes on to say, "The Smithsonian had insect cases that the Farm entomologist really liked, but thought we couldn't afford. However, it turned out that when some of the Farm entomologists made inquiries about these cases, the plans for them belonged to the Smithsonian, not the American manufacturer. The Smithsonian entomologists offered to let Agriculture Canada have the plans for free so that we could look for a Canadian manufacturer capable of fabricating them. So, I set up a small committee of entomologists to investigate this possibility. They were finally able to locate a manufacturer in Quebec City who could produce the cases to the Smithsonian's specifications at about a quarter of the price that we would have had to pay to buy them from the American manufacturer." The steel cases were finally delivered in January of 1985. This story is also noteworthy in confirming that all interactions with the Institute entomologist weren't adversarial. This would have been a very popular process and outcome for the entomologists.

Once new entomological storage cases were obtained, my father turned his attention to storage conditions for the National plant herbarium. He says, "The storage for plant specimens was also a real problem. The botanical collection was stored in slotted steel cases in the Saunders Building, a building specifically designed with reinforced floors to support the heavy cases. This is also the reason the botanists continued to be housed in the Saunders Building while the rest of the Institute was located in the Neatby Building. The problem was that as the collection got larger and larger, it reached the stage that there was no more room in the herbarium. They started to store specimens wherever they could find space, including the hallways. They were even thinking about putting some of the collection in other buildings." The dispersal of the collection was resolved with the acquisition and installation of compactors in January of 1986. Plant compactors are automated back-to-back, rolling shelves that allow just enough space to access the needed specimen in the row in which the specimen is located. You only have to press a button to have the shelves open at the specified location. My father says, "With this system, we could store about three times the number of specimens compared to the old cases." It is a much more efficient use of limited space. Since the collection could now be compacted, they have been able to continue adding to the collection without worrying about where to put the material.

When my father became Director, he became interested in further justifying the value of his Institute by producing information that would be useful to the public. He really put a lot of pressure to become more applied on scientists who were only interested in their scientific publications and career advancement. Many of them had a lot of information that was useful to the public within their areas of expertise. He would continually remind them that they were accountable to taxpayers and if there was something useful, they should get it out there were it could be used. For instance, he made some of the entomologists working on beetles produce an information manual on the identification of beetles that damage grains. This would be useful information for farmers or grain purchasers. They also produced a manual on bark beetles that would cause problems to trees by getting underneath the bark or beetles that ate fungal spores, which would lead to the spread of diseases. This information would be useful to the forestry and tree nursery industries.

Certainly, he practiced what he preached. As part of their submission in nominating my father for the Lawson Medal, Stephen Darbyshire and Suzanne Warwick did a great job of summarizing his contributions to the non-scientific community:

> Gerry's research and expertise on weeds reached the general Canadian public, as well as many people outside the research community, through (several) important publications. It is hard to measure the profound impact that these publications have had on the lay public and professionals outside of botanical science, but all of these titles are still in print (in one form or another), in both English and French, having gone through various updates

and/or reprintings.

Weeds of Canada was published with Clarence Frankton by the federal Department of Agriculture. It succeeded an earlier edition but has remained in print under this title and Gerry's authorship, with updates and reprinting, since 1970. This publication has been the single most important identification guide for Canadian agricultural weeds for decades.

Common weeds of Canada/Les mauvaises herbes communes du Canada was first published in 1976 and contained many of Gerry's excellent photographs of weeds, rather than the line drawings in *Weeds of Canada*. ... This small book appealed to the general public and was extremely popular. It can be found on bookshelves of botanists, farmers and gardeners across the country.

Among the most misunderstood plants in Canada are those of the genus *Toxicodendron*. The small and clearly written booklet on poison ivy and its relatives, written by Gerry and published by the Department of Agriculture in both languages, has provided straightforward science-based information on this plant for Canadians for more than two decades. This booklet has been of use to untold numbers of doctors and dermatitis sufferers in Canada and the USA. It has no doubt helped many professionals and non-professionals alike to make identifications and diagnoses. It has probably helped equally in preventing mis-diagnosis of rhus dermatitis in areas outside the plant's ranges. Although not available in printed form any more, the web-based version receives tremendous traffic. Also ground breaking and equally important to the medical and agricultural communities were his extensive compilations on Poisonous Plants in Canada.

My father always felt it was his duty to take on this type of endeavour. Most of the things my father took on, he did because he enjoyed doing it. "It was satisfying providing information that was useful to the public, and not just the scientific community. I think that some of the scientists I pestered to produce applied information for the public probably ended up getting personal satisfaction out of this type of work as well." This is what also drove him to set up a weed website in his 70s, which he still actively manages today at 86 and counting. There is no monetary benefit to him. Most people accessing the information don't even know who he is.

My father was always receptive to special initiatives that would add value to the Institute. During his time as Director, he was involved in several different focused hiring initiatives. Every now and then, an idea would come down from senior management or federal politicians to encourage the hiring of a special interest group. They would inform managers that they would be able to access additional funds to accomplish these special initiatives. These ideas typically applied to Research Branches across Canada. My father was always on the lookout for extra money for his Institute. There were always many things staff wanted and needed but never enough money. He always expressed an interest in these programs. They would ask, "How much could you use?" His response was always, "How much do you have?" Unbelievably, most of the time, he was the only manager, across Canada, that seized these opportunities. All of these special programs had many problems. My father comments, "Most Directors didn't want to take these programs on because they were so difficult. I always took it as a challenge."

In one instance, they retained handicapped workers to prepare specimens in all the sections of the Institute. There were actually two separate programs offered by the Institute. The first program, begun in 1980, hired homebound handicap persons to prepare specimen materials. This program was renewed over a number of years. However, my father continually struggled with repeated, last-minute confirmation of annual funding of the program, and the threatened cancellation of provincial subsidies.

✍ April 19, 1982 – Convinced Morrison to give us $20,000 for homebound handicapped but I am fed up with begging every year and I am going to write him for a permanent commitment or I am going to drop the program as of April 1, 1983 so that participants can be notified early and make appropriate arrangements

☒ May 7, 1982 – Morrison caved into my pressure and granted us money for homebound handicapped in the future.

These were two-year term positions that unfortunately didn't pay very much. In spite of that, there were handicapped people that wanted the jobs, because they wanted to work. They liked to feel worthwhile. The second program, which involved people coming into the office to work, only lasted for one year. Not everyone had the ability or means to come to the Institute. Transportation was a problem for many of the handicapped workers. Once again, the workers that came to the Institute were mainly hired to prepare specimen materials. However, because they were working within the Institute, once they demonstrated their abilities to their colleagues, they were invariably dragged into doing other tasks. "People are always looking for help," my father says. In one case, a participant was a good and keen worker. When a technician job opening came up, totally unrelated to the handicapped program, he applied and because he had the experience and was a known quantity, he got the job. In fact, this person only recently retired after many years in the position. The opportunity allowed him to demonstrate his abilities and put him in the position to take advantage of a further opportunity.

Participants of both programs had problems with the impact of entering the workforce on the disability benefits they were receiving. If they worked and earned a certain level of income, their benefits were terminated. The candidates were understandingly always nervous about taking the positions because they would not be earning much more than what they had been getting. My father tells me, "They didn't even mind losing the benefits, but when the term finished these workers had a terrible time getting back their benefits. It sometimes took six months to a year to get back their benefits again. They certainly were not rewarded for trying to become self-sufficient."

Yet another cost-effective program was developed in association with Parks Canada. The Institute arranged to conduct inventories of organisms in various national parks across Canada. "The previous Director, Dave Hardwick, initiated an idea, which I implemented in a big way," my father says. A team, including an entomologist, a mycologist, and a vascular plant taxonomist would conduct visits to a particular park. They would each collect specimens of their specialty. They would then be responsible for writing a report. They would highlight findings that they thought the park naturalists should know about, things that were special in the park. This was valuable information in developing interpretive programs. The work on each park usually took place over a couple of years. During the time my father was Director of the Biosystematics Research Institute four parks were completed, one in Manitoba, one in Southern Ontario, one in New Brunswick, and one in the Cape Breton Highlands of Nova Scotia.

"It didn't cost the Institute anything, and for just the cost of expenses Parks Canada received all this scientific expertise," my father says. Agriculture Canada also ended up with a tremendous collection of organisms from these national parks that they never had before. My father comments, "It was a big help in building the National Collection. Staff also used to love doing the work. They got to spend time in amazing natural areas." The individual scientists also had the right to use any scientific information that they learned in carrying out their research work.

The ultimate testament to my father's desire to showcase the Biosystematics Research Institute was his idea to document the history of systematics in Agriculture Canada at the Central Experimental Farm as the Institute's centennial project. While the centennial of the experimental farm system was 1887 to

1987, the systematics at the Central Experimental Farm in Ottawa actually started one year before. They acknowledged this by documenting the history of systematics between 1886 and 1986. My father was the driving force behind the publication *Systematics in Agriculture Canada at Ottawa 1886–1986*. He selected Bill Cody in botany, Douglas Savile in mycology, and Michael Sarazin in entomology to write the respective sections for each of their disciplines. In addition to writing the forward, my father reviewed and edited this historical document. He changed quite a bit of the material for botany and mycology. As with many other similar initiatives, my father's primary interested at the time was just getting it done. He was never given much credit for it. He comments, "In hindsight, it annoys me, but at the time it didn't occur to me."

16
FRENCH IN THE PUBLIC SERVICE

In typical style, my father dealt with the introduction of bilingualism into the federal public service as he did everything else, in a positive manner.

At one time, if you were French, you were looked down on. It limited employment opportunities. The first language of my grandfather, Wilfred Mulligan, was French. However, he never spoke it at work. My father also remembers his administrative officer, Andre Giroux, telling him once that it was his goal when he joined the federal public service to try to speak English so well that no one would know that he was French. He thought that this would allow for better advancement opportunities. My father acknowledges that it was a terrible situation. However, he also laments that the situation seems to have swung the other way now. "I have been around long enough to learn that it is always the same; it is one group or another that tries to take control," he says.

In 1967, the *Official Languages Act* was adopted in Canada. By the early 1970s, bilingualism in the federal public service was starting to play a significant role. My father was already Assistant Director in 1973 when bilingualism requirements were adopted in the federal government. On February 1, 1974, my father proactively began a course of self-teaching French using the Berlitz language system. Virtually every day, he would get up early, between five and five-thirty in the morning, to study for an hour before leaving for work. In studying French grammar, my father learned something many of us who learn a second language learn, "In all the years that I took English at school, I never learned about all the tenses, such as conditional. I now know more about French grammar than I do about English grammar."

- August 28, 1974 – I finished Berlitz-Français for the second time. Start records tomorrow.

- October 29, 1974 – Marg bought me advanced French. The record seems unbelievably fast. I can understand almost nothing.

- March 16, 1975 – I am trying to learn how to understand French conversation by concentrating on records. I can read fairly well now but my comprehension of conversation is virtually nil.

- March 12, 1976 – comprehension of French conversation is very small a year later.

- July 14, 1976 - I received notice today that I passed my French level 3344 and my level is 4444. I started Feb. 1, 1974, so it took me 2 years, 5 months and thirteen days of my time to reach my level. I only missed 5 days total. I may not be bright, but I have lots of perseverance.

Senior management would not support my father in taking any courses on government time and expense. This does not surprise me. I have often seen this phenomenon. If you are too competent and productive, management does not want to lose you to language training. Eventually, he managed to meet the language levels for his position in writing and grammar, but not for speaking. He did it almost all on his own and on his own time.

⌚ September 18, 1975 – Hardwick and I discussed my going on French half days. He was not keen. I am.

⌚ September 29, 1975 – Hardwick phoned this morning to say that he is not going to let me go on half-time French. Does this mean that Hardwick has decided to Grandfather himself and get a French Assistant Director?

⌚ July 13, 1976 – I was phoned about a French test just after I got to work. The test is tomorrow at 9 am. Not much warning. I went home and tried to study. I am very apprehensive.

⌚ July 14, 1976 – Went for French test. I did very poorly in reading, too slow and I did not nearly finish in time. I think that I did pretty well on writing. Did very poorly on listening comprehension. I should have looked at answers first and then listened to questions. I think I did as well as I could have on speaking. It will be interesting if I pass writing and speaking but failed the other two.

⌚ September 16, 1976 – I went to my first session of conversational French. I probably am the worst of four in the class.

⌚ February 1, 1977 – third year of French.[5]

One of the early proposals to fast track French workers into the public service was with unilingual French cells.

⌚ September 15, 1975 – Mountain met with Directors regarding unilingual French cells in the Institute.

⌚ October 1, 1975 – Heard on radio today about all francophone units in the National Capital Region.

⌚ October 2, 1975 – CFRA is spearheading quite a lot of protest about French unilingual units.

By the time he became Director in 1980, bilingualism began to be enforced more strictly. As the incumbent in the position, my

---

[5] He passed his level during the past year without taking the course. He has been taking a 1.5-hour course, Monday and Friday for 3 months. This improved his comprehension and speaking.

father had incumbent rights.

✍ November 27, 1979 – Received letter today from bilingualism saying that I do not have to take French as Director.

✍ January 4, 1980 – Finished reading my third French book in less than three weeks, my first three books.

✍ April 1, 1980 – I was phoned for French today and I told them that I was going to take the grandfather clause.

✍ August 12, 1980 – Pressure to hire francophones.

✍ August 13, 1980 – Talked to Campbell and Smith regarding francophone representation for scientists and recruiting francophone *lepidopterist* and *acarologist*.

✍ August 15, 1980 – We hired a francophone artist today. Decided today to hire francophones except for exceptional scientists available.

In 1981, there was a directive to increase the number of francophone scientists in the federal public service. All the directors across Canada were told that Agriculture Canada would give them the person years and budget to hire them. My father was asked how many he wanted. Six. How many did he get? Six. No one else requested any.

Once they received approval for six positions for their Institute, my father gathered some of the francophone scientists currently on staff and asked them to contact universities throughout the Province of Quebec to see if they could identify potential candidates. Only two of the candidates met the educational requirements and had an interest in relevant fields of study. In the end, they received permission to identify good students who had already earned their undergraduate degree and were willing to specialize in the group of insects or plants identified as gaps at the Institute. The four selected students were then sent to university at government expense.

✍ May 21, 1981 - Met with Lindquist, Campbell, Baum, Smith,

Giroux and people from our personnel to figure out how to handle bringing our French BIs (Biologists) to Ottawa and sending them off to university.

My father ran into a lot of difficulty after he decided to pursue the hiring of francophone scientists. He received poison pen letters against his support of francophone scientists, mostly from Alberta. One of them was from George Ball, professor and Chair of the Entomology Department at the University of Edmonton. He was furious about it. He even wrote an article in the journal of the Entomological Society of Canada blasting my father, who responded with an article of his own in rebuttal.

Ø April 14, 1981– Many entomologists are writing in as a result of a letter in *Entomological Society Bulletin* regarding French essential positions.

Ø August 18, 1981 – Davis telephoned from McMasters to tell me that my letter will be in the next entomology bulletin.

Ø February 16, 1982 – Saw a piece from Calgary paper regarding French essential biologists and criticizing BRI. This is the result of our Bulletin.

As it turned out, Jean-François Landry, one of the francophone candidates they selected to work on *Lepidoptera* was sent to obtain his PhD under the supervision of George Ball. My father laughs when he says that Ball changed his mind completely once he worked with Landry. Ball grudgingly told my father, "Well, if they're all like Landry, it's okay." My father wasn't surprised to hear this. They had done their homework in selecting those they hired for these positions.

Another success story was Yolande Dalpé, a mycologist. The Institute had wanted someone to work on mycorrhizal fungi, which have a symbiotic relationship with plants, resulting in increased plant productivity. This was a new field of research at the time, and they didn't have anyone working in this area. These mycorrhizal fungi are important for many crops, especially many cereal crops, that do better if there are certain mycorrhizal fungi growing in association with the roots to assist in uptake. When they first approached her, Dalpé was nearing completion of her PhD. Agriculture Canada helped her finish her post-graduate education in their field of interest and bring that knowledge to the Institute.

Of the six scientists hired because of this program, five turned out well, with only one a disappointment. As of 2010, they are all still working for the Research Branch, somewhere in Canada. The one disappointment was a plant taxonomist the Institute selected to work on the area dearest to my father's heart. The Institute wanted someone to work on the mustard family, a very important plant family, as there was no one working on it at the time. They hired a student and supported him for three years while he went to work under a professor in Belgium who was a specialist on the mustard family. Unfortunately, once he received his PhD and returned to Canada, he didn't work for very long on what he was hired for. He decided he wasn't interest in working on the mustard family.

As time went on, the public service continued to raise the language levels. My father became Acting Director General for six months in 1986 when Dr. Jack Morrison had to take a leave of absence to deal with a health problem. My father had taken on this position on many occasions over the years. He believes that he would have been confirmed permanently in the position if he had been more bilingual. This was the first time that bilingualism had become an impediment to his advancement. He doesn't think he would have done nearly as well under the present system of official bilingualism, even with a PhD.

17
NUISANCE PLANTS

Most of the time, plants contribute positively to people's quality of life. Weeds by definition are unwanted plants. However, some plants can go way beyond being unwanted and become a real nuisance when they become the cause of hay fever, rashes, and other allergic reactions. As a weed scientist, my father has had a lot of experience dealing with nuisance plant issues over the years, in some cases personally.

One of his pet peeves is that "the scientific community has known for a long time that ragweed is the most problematic plant species in Canada causing hay fever. Unfortunately, there is a persistent ongoing myth that *Solidago* more commonly known as Goldenrod is the culprit. This is because it flowers at the same time as ragweed. Goldenrod's bright yellow flowers are the ones noticeable in the landscape. Even people who should know better help in perpetuating this myth."

Another myth is communicated by pharmaceutical companies selling hay fever medication. The huge colourful flowers of species such as hibiscus provide a much better visual for their advertising campaigns than the innocuous green flowers of ragweed. These commercials drive my father crazy. As soon as one of these ads comes on the screen, my family knows we are in for a rant on just how wrong the information is. My father has never been able to restrain himself from commenting, "They use large colourful flowers and stamens with sticky pollen. During ragweed season, if you hit a clump of ragweed, a huge drift of pollen is released into the air. If you hit a hibiscus flower, nothing will happen to the pollen. It won't go anywhere. This type of flower is insect pollinated." He goes on to explain that the pollen on showy blossoms has evolved to be sticky so that it sticks on the insects that visit the flower. "Hay fever plants, like ragweed, are most likely to be the greenest flowers. Insects are not attracted to them. Therefore, they have to rely on wind pollination. Conversely, plants with colourful flowers with sticky pollen aren't wind pollinated. It would be a waste of their resources to expend the large amount of energy required to produce brilliant flowers if they were wind pollinated. Wind pollinated plants tend to have poor individual flowers, but a much, much larger amount of pollen than those pollinated by insects. It has been shown scientifically, using tagged bees, that there is a tendency when bees are gathering nectar, for them to go to similar plants in an area. Therefore, insect pollinated flowers will have a high probability of having their pollen moved to the same species a short time later. On the other hand, wind distributed pollen is not discriminating on where it lands. Consequently wind pollinated plants need to produce a lot of pollen to increase the probability that their pollen lands on the same plant species."

John Bassett made a career out of studying hay fever. "It was his specialty," my father says. Bassett produced a pollen atlas for Canada in 1978. The pollen atlas describes and identifies pollen for most of the plants in Canada known to cause hay fever. My father describes the process he used: "Bassett would travel to fire stations across Canada in the mid-1970s where he would install a pollen gathering device on the top of the station to collect windblown pollen. The firemen would be paid by Agriculture Canada for changing the slides, sometimes every

day. The firemen would use the money for their coffee or
recreation fund. Most of the stations were happy to be involved.
The firemen would send Bassett the slides in boxes supplied by
Agriculture Canada. Bassett then would examine the slides for
windblown pollen. He would not be looking to identify all the
pollen on the slide; he would be looking for certain types of
pollen, such as ragweed pollen. From this accumulated
information, Bassett produced a valuable annual information
bulletin called *Canadian Havens from Hay Fever*. This listed places
in Canada with little or no ragweed pollen. He worked in
partnership with Health and Welfare Canada. They would fund
and distribute the brochures." If hay fever is a problem, and
you're willing to move to get away from the problem, you might
want to consult one of John Bassett's publications.

I for one have been a frequent victim of another plant, poison
ivy. Growing up, I always seemed to be much more sensitive to
the effects of the oil on my skin than my brothers were. It
didn't matter that I could identify it from a young age. If you
walk through it, break the plant, and expose the oils, it may
cause you problems; the plant must be broken to cause the rash.
It is reported, and my father thinks it is reasonable to believe,
that people tend to get poison ivy rashes more frequently in the
spring, when the leaves are very tender and bruise easily.
Further on in the growing season, the plant tissue gets tougher.
Growing up, I remember my father talking about the time
someone came in carrying a poison ivy plant for identification.
Holding out the plant in their hands, they asked him, "Is this
poison ivy?" When he confirmed, that indeed it was poison ivy,
they dropped it like a hot potato.

Biologist E. Grant Anderson completed the first poison ivy
(*Rhus radicans*) publication produced by Agriculture Canada in
the late 1940s. My father expanded on this work. He did some
original research on poison ivy by looking at their chromosomes
and crossing the different varieties. As usual, he always carried it
further than what had been previously done. In the course of

this work, he also described a new variety of poison ivy. My father's poison ivy information has always been very popular with the public. Unfortunately, the paper version of the poison ivy brochure is no longer produced and the web information has disappeared from the Agriculture and Agri-Foods Canada website. He tried numerous times to get the information reinstated, to no avail. Finally, my father decided to rewrite the information and include it on his personal website. He also added poison sumac and western poison oak to the information. One of the things that he tried to clarify was the belief that poison oak is widespread in Canada. In fact, the only poison oak in Canada is found along the west coast on a couple of small islands around Vancouver Island. When you get down into California, poison oak is the main rash-causing plant.

My father comments, "The media is not helpful in dispelling plant myths. When they get a hold of a plant story, they tend to embellish the details and generally get the facts wrong. Unfortunately, people tend to believe the media account. A perfect example is 2010 stories on Giant Hogweed (*Heracleum mantegazzianum*). The media hyped the plant out of all proportion to problems associated with it. The media chose to focus on the fact that you could be blinded by Giant Hogweed." As far as my father knows, there has never been a case of anyone being blinded by the oil from Giant Hogweed. He thinks a reporter probably asked, "Could you be blinded if you got oil in your eyes?" When someone replied, "Yes, you probably could," that became the focus of the story. In July 2010, the *National Post* was one of many newspapers that heralded headlines such as, "Giant weed that burns and blinds spreads across Canada." My father is quick to point out that "Giant Hogweed is not very common in Canada, so the chances of the ordinary person coming into contact with it are very low, so low that it is not even worth worrying about. If you encounter it, you would have to break part of the plant to be exposed to the oil or sap. Then it requires the oil on your skin to be exposed to sunlight in order to activate the rash." In response to the media reaction, one of my father's colleagues, Stephen Darbyshire, purposely broke open a Giant Hogweed plant and rubbed the oil on his arm to see what type of rash would develop. A big red, blistery rash resulted. My father took a picture and posted it on his weed website. Scientific curiosity can certainly lead to some odd behaviour sometimes!

My father goes on to say, "There is another plant, Wild Parsnip (*Pastinaca sativa*), that is much smaller, but a lot more common than Giant Hogweed. It is in the same family as Giant Hogweed, and has the same chemical in its oil that causes a rash. The media could be helpful in alerting people about this plant." There was a case that my father is aware of where a female summer student ran into a lot of trouble with this plant. He says, "She was clearing brush with a whipper snipper and unfortunately went into a stand of wild parsnip. She was not wearing any protective clothing, just regular summer clothes with lots of exposed skin. As a result, she got oil all over her skin and ended up in the hospital. The oil in wild parsnip is not as powerful as the oil in Giant Hogweed, but it is much more common, so even if the oil is weaker in strength, you are more likely to be exposed to more of it. Even the umbels and seeds can give you a rash."

Early in his career, my father carried out some research on Yarrow (*Achillea*). Most people know the introduced species and ornamental cultivars, with a yellow or reddish flower, used as a garden perennial, but there are also several native yarrow species. As part of his research, my father collected many clones of yarrow from various areas, grew them, examined them and made chromosome counts of them all. He was one of the first botanists to discover that the *Achillea* viewed as a common weed in Canada was not an introduced species, but a native species with a different chromosome number. "In doing all this work, I was handling *Achillea* quite a bit. I finally reached the stage, after about a year, where my eyes started to puff up so much that they were almost closed," he says. At that point, he couldn't handle *Achillea* anymore. My father had to enlist the assistance of John Bassett to help him finish his work. He made Bassett a coauthor of the paper on this research: Mulligan, G.A. and Bassett, I.J. 1959. "Achillea millefolium complex in Canada and portions of the United States" published in the *Canadian Journal of Botany*.

My father soon found out that he was not only allergic to *Achillea*, but he had become sensitized to quite a number of plants in the same family. He had worked on *Chrysanthemum leucanthemum* in 1958, which also would have contributed to the development of this sensitivity. When he travelled out west, through sagebrush country, he also had problems in areas with extensive growth of *Artemisia*. He developed the sensitivity with one genus in the family, but whatever the problem component was, it was present in quite a number of genera in the family. Thereafter, he could not work on many plants in the *Compositae* family any more. Unfortunately, it was difficult to avoid them. Time and time again, my father's diaries document the results of his exposure to them:

- August 10, 1983 – My eyes are puffed up from *Compositae* and any skin, especially on my face is very itchy.

- May 19, 1984 – My eyes are sore, itchy and swollen with my old allergy.

- September 17, 1985 – My eyes are still sore and face itchy and swollen from the chrysanthemums I picked on the 14th.

My father's allergic reaction to plants in the *Compositae* family sent him in new research directions. He started doing a lot of research with mustards (*Brassicaceae*). Luckily, he has never had any difficulty with plants in this family. When I ask if any of his colleagues developed similar sensitivities to plants they studied, he admits that he has never discussed the topic with them. He is aware that individuals working in the horticultural industry have developed allergies to plants that they handle frequently. "One of the most famous examples," he says, "is tulip thumb, which affects workers in Holland who handle a lot of tulip bulbs. They get a swollen thumb. To allow them to keep on working, they must wear gloves. In addition, outside workers who are frequently exposed to poison ivy are known to develop an increasing sensitivity to the oil. Many of these workers are not even aware that this is happening. They know it is getting worse, but don't understand the reason." So knowing the cause is the first step in avoiding the problem.

18
GENETICALLY MODIFIED

Several topics are guaranteed to get my father riled up. People ranting about the evils of genetically modified food is one of them. It's not that he doesn't have his own concerns about genetic manipulation it's just that he finds that more often than not people have their facts wrong.

In 1984, my father successfully lobbied for the set-up of a gene pool in the Biosystematics Research Institute at the Central Experimental Farm. He states, "The purpose of this gene pool was to collect and store viable seed of all the different cultivated plant varieties. The goal was to have genes with as much genetic variability as possible within such species as wheat, oats, or apples. This would enable a plant breeder who was looking for a particular trait in a new variety, to have access to a broad range of raw material. A gene pool would allow this material to be available for plant breeders in perpetuity."

Agriculture Canada started to collect material for the gene pool. My father tells me, "The department actually sent a group of scientists from the Farm to the Middle East to collect land races from various cereals, such as wheat and oats, to use in plant breeding. They were primarily interested in collecting oat populations of land races that had various characteristics, such as resistance to rust, a more upright structure or the ability to keep their kernels."

Land races in this context, are wild populations of cultivated plants. My father explains, "Over many years these cultivated plants have been selected out for specific characteristic of interest to local people. In a region, there may be all sorts of land races, as various tribes or cultures have selected them for different characteristics. Many of these land races have been disappearing, because developed countries have produced varieties of cultivated plants with higher yields. They have convinced many of these cultures to grow the new cultivars instead of their traditional land races. With the disappearance of land races, a valuable gene pool is also being lost. This is a concern of geneticists. It has already become a problem because some cultivars propagate genetically identical plants over vast areas of agricultural lands. With such uniformity, a disease could wipe out huge areas of cropland."

However, with changes in plant breeding techniques, many gene pools have been abandoned. Most plant breeders no longer use land races because it is a time consuming job to collect, propagate, breed, and select them. The collected seed only remains viable for a certain length of time. Gene pools have to place the seed under various types of cold treatment to extend its viability. They would also have to use some of the seed continually for the propagation of plants to produce new seed that could be placed back in the gene pool. This is not being done any more, so any collected material has now become obsolete.

Historically, plant breeding was carried out almost exclusively between individuals of the same species or closely related species. However, advances in plant breeding have changed things. Now, if plant breeders want a new variety, they can transfer gene fragments from organisms that aren't even in the plant kingdom; for example, taking gene fragments from a mouse and putting it into a wheat plant to produce a certain characteristic in the wheat plant. This transfer of genes is done in the lab. This is what some people refer to as genetically modified food, but what my father calls "genetic engineering." He says, "There is a great lack of understanding of the difference between genetic modification and genetic engineering. Everything is genetically modified. All new varieties have been produced by genetically modifying the species."

My father recounts a recent visit to a natural food store to buy some granola for my mother. When he went up to the counter to pay for his purchase the cashier asked, "Would you mind signing this petition?" My father responded by asking her what the petition was about. She showed him the petition, which read, "I am in favour of banning all genetically modified food." The cashier added, "I'd like you to sign it because we want to stop people buying genetically modified food." My father replied, "Do you really want me to sign this? Everything you have in your store here is genetically modified." "Oh no!" was her horrified reply. "Well it is," he said. He didn't pursue the issue any further than that and left the store. "She didn't know what she was talking about. Everything in the store was genetically modified, just by a different technique than she was referring to," he comments.

That said, my father is sympathetic to concerns about genetic engineering. A good example is genetically engineered canola. He explains, "One of the problems with canola, which is a *Brassicaceae* related to cabbage, is that it is subject to many insect pests. To deal with this, they have taken a gene fragment from an animal and put it in canola. This has produced a canola plant that is no longer attacked by these pests. They have also put a gene taken from another organism that will allow canola to be sprayed with herbicides and insecticides without killing the plant. The problem with this is that it now enables them to use a lot more chemicals on fields than they were able to do with old plant breeding techniques. Because of this, the soil gets more contaminated. Both the canola plants and other crops planted in the fields will then uptake these chemicals into their plant tissue."

"In the United States, they are also running into difficulty with some crops due to the genetic uniformity resulting from genetic engineering. When previously unknown diseases are encountered, it can wipe out big swaths of cropland because there is a lot of vulnerability associated with this uniformity," my father says. He finds that most of the articles he reads and most of the people he hears talking against genetically modified foods don't zero in on the real problems associated with genetic engineering.

People who are against genetic engineering don't want the products of genetic engineering to be consumed. They believe it is bad for their health. My father asserts, "Consumption of genetically engineered food is not the main problem. The main problem is that genetic engineering is destroying gene pools." In the future, he predicts that the agricultural industry is going to encounter great difficulty with the demise of gene pools. "They are going to have to rely on genetic engineering. This could end up being very limiting," he laments. At a time when climate change is necessitating planners in many industries to start building in greater resiliency, the consequences of genetic engineering seem to be going in exactly the opposite direction.

19
FAMILY MAN

Rosanna (Menchini) Carson, my father's executive secretary, has always been one of his biggest fans. She pinpoints one of the reasons for their positive relationship to that fact that "he was a family man. I only ever heard your father say good things about you and your brothers," she says. "I also thought it was nice to know about parents that actually loved each other. In this day and age, it was really good to see. I always respected your father for his dedication to his family." One story she tells is about an incident when she first started dating her husband, Bruce Carson. She met him at work when he was managing a project in the Neatby Building. "When Bruce came to take me out for coffee, your father would be sitting at his desk with his glasses perched on his nose checking him out," reports Carson. Bruce would say, "Oh god, it's almost like your father!" Carson loved it. Later, my father told her, "He seems like a nice guy Rosanna." Carson crows, "I got the seal of approval!"

For his entire career, my father always enjoyed going home for lunch with his family. "I found it to be a wonderful experience. I was lucky to have a good family relationship. We all got along well and I enjoyed doing things with my four children," he says. I remember this as a unique and special thing that none of my friend's fathers did. Until we all reached high school, the whole family ate all three meals together. My father believes that his whole career would not have been possible if he had not been able to go home and talk over some of the troubles he was having at work. This was particularly true once he became Director of the Biosystematics Research Institute; a big part of his success was that my mother, Margaret, provided him with a safe haven. Discussing problems and issues with the family gave my father a sounding board that allowed him to figure out better approaches to dealing with situations that arose. This resulted in him being able to return to work in the afternoon in a much better frame of mind. "I would lay all the morning's problems on poor Margaret and get rid of my frustrations. I vividly remember when I was offered the job as Director. I didn't want it and tried to get out of it. I came home and talked it over with her." He had told the Director General that he would think about it. However, in his typical decisive style, "I only thought about it overnight."

I was curious to know what my father's colleagues at the Farm thought about him going home for lunch every day. It was Carson's recollection that it made no impression on the scientists, but that some of the administrative staff made fun of it, with snide comments like, "Who goes home for lunch? Who wants to be with the wife for lunch?" But Carson says, "I thought it was wonderful that he did it. I could see the change in him."

My youngest brother, Paul, was the only child still living at home during the bulk of the time that my father was Director of the Institute. Paul recently told my father that what he heard during our parents' mealtime discussions formulated many of the things he uses in his job as Head of Global Compensation in human resources for the technology company Alcatel-Lucent. "I remember Dad having a strong ethical streak in his management of the Institute. This did not necessarily come out on the day-to-day issues, but at certain critical points, there would be a time at which he had to make a decision. He would take a principled decision, the ethical position, or the common man's position. I like to think that this is something that I have carried on in my own management style."

Paul says that he used to be enthralled by all the stories about what was going on at work. "I remember Dad talking to Mom about the personnel dynamics at work. Bernard Baum loomed large in the conversation, but there were other names that I got to know very well over time. All the drama and politics at the office was like a soap opera with the same cast of characters. The latest developments in the plot unfolded over time. I used to look forward to hearing about it."

We have all said similar things. My parents are amazed. They were completely unaware that we were even listening. As soon as my father would walk through the door my mother would greet him with, "What's new? You must have something for me." Initially, he would often say, "Nothing," but she would persist. Eventually, he would end up recounting his morning or afternoon. He always had interesting things to impart.

My middle brother, Steve, says that the main impact that hearing all Dad's stories had on him was that it made him decide that working for the government was something he wouldn't want to do. My mother is surprised that Steve would have even thought along those lines at such a young age. Having the experience of managing staff in the high technology sector, Steve feels that the normal difficulties of dealing with staff are amplified in government. "It wasn't a conscious decision to avoid it, but I certainly didn't seek it out." It is interesting that all this workplace drama had such polar opposite effects on Paul and Steve.

What still amazes my oldest brother, Don, about my father, is how he just gets on with things. "He gets things done. His motto is, just do it!" Don feels that he is just like that at work. "There is a sense of urgency, without being overbearing. If you've got something to do, don't put it off, just get it done, and move onto the next thing. He has instilled this in all of us more than anything," he says. I would certainly have to agree with Don. Whether it's genetic, learned, or a combination of both, I too am one to be quick and decisive and to get things done without a lot of delay.

One of the things that Don really appreciated about our parents was that they were never negative. He says, "They were consistently supportive and never got in the way if you wanted to try something. We went to summer camps, we played all kinds of sports, and we went on family trips to various places. There was no allowance for whining. It was "We can do it. Let's explore." Many people just stayed in the same house their whole life, especially in the era in which we grew up. Our parents weren't like that." When we outgrew the bungalow on Erindale Drive, we moved up the street to a bigger house. There were two more moves after that as the family dynamics continued to change. They rented or owned a series of cottages as it suited their needs. We went on fieldtrips with my father to the Gaspé Peninsula and Banff National Park. There was a lot of variety in what we did as a family. My father agrees. "For the time, we did a lot more and a lot of different things than most of our neighbours. Of course it doesn't compare with what the grandkids are doing these days!"

My youngest brother, Paul, believes that although we obviously have great parents, they weren't perfect. He surprises me by acknowledging, "I wasn't necessarily always easy to deal with, so they got mad at me a lot. There were certainly times of conflict. But you don't tend to dwell on those times. You remember the good times. I spent a lot of time with them on various pieces of land they owned. They would drag me out cross-country skiing or golfing, usually at some crazy early time in the morning. Many times, we golfed in the rain. I hated it at the time, but now I look back fondly on those experiences." Steve comments along a similar vein, "While I liked going places, like the hobby farm, it wasn't always what I wanted to do." He does acknowledge that, with the exception of attending church, in the end he always enjoyed it once he got there.

Steve also quite rightly observes, "We got our good work ethic and ability to manage money from our parents." Through hard work, good saving and spending practices, my brothers and I have all managed to get through university on our own dime with no or minimal debt. As personal debt has reached crisis levels throughout North America, we have continued to buck the norm thanks to the good example and good advice of our parents.

"Keep your options open" was one of the most often repeated mantras we heard from our father throughout our lives. While at the time you wanted to respond with an exasperated, "Yeah, yeah, yeah," it was invariably good advice. Whether it was what courses to take in high school in preparation for university, change of job strategies, or other important life decisions, you could be expected to hear this comment often and repeatedly. I will never live down, in my father's eyes, dropping physics in grade thirteen. This was a cardinal sin with respect to keeping your options open. I still hear about it to this day!

One of the things that always impressed Carson about my father was that there were no airs about him. "I always felt relaxed around him." I agree. My father has never been an intellectual snob. He always taught his kids to take people at face value. It wasn't until I went away to university that I fully appreciated the family that I had. When you live in such a small, uniform world growing up, it is very easy to believe that everyone else lives as you do. While I loved being exposed to the much, much greater cultural and socio-economic diversity of life on the University of Toronto campus, hearing about other people's family dynamics was a real revelation for me.

After hearing many of our comments, my father says, "In the last few years, your mother and I have frequently talked about how pleased we are with the way that all of our children have turned out. It is really the greatest satisfaction that Marg and I have in our old age. When you see all the problems that other families have, it makes you appreciate it even more. We can't understand how you all did so well, because we were so inexperienced. We didn't know anything about parenting. Even though I am so disillusioned with religion now, maybe it gave us a core set of values to work with. Maybe this is the good part about religion. In any case, we are so proud of you all."

A big part of their success as parents was to "lead by example." I also remember my parents once telling me that they tried hard to present a unified front to their children. If they disagreed on something, they tried to hash it out behind the scenes before addressing it with us. Paul echoes similar sentiments, "We were always a close family, with no drama. They were supportive and interested in your schoolwork and other activities. They were always talking about politics and other world events. It was a good family atmosphere. They were just nice people."

20
MORE THAN A SCIENTIST

While my father certainly enjoyed his work, it was far from the only important thing in his life. His diverse interests almost certainly helped him cope with the many aggravations and challenges he faced as both a scientist and manager, and later would enable a seamless transition into retirement.

Sports have always been a big part of my father's life, as they have for my entire family. My father played a lot of hockey growing up. At Macdonald College, he played on and coached many inter-class teams. Actually, "I played on every team, including track, volleyball, and water polo," my father says. In his first two years at Macdonald College, he played varsity hockey. He was under pressure to play football, but he didn't want to play two varsity sports at the same time. In his final year, he played varsity football instead of hockey. When my father looks back, he shakes his head and says, "Playing football was a bad decision. I was always a lean guy. I didn't have the bulk to play football." He has some physical injuries from playing football that still haunt him today. My brother, Don, remembers Dad telling him that his function on the varsity football team was returning punts. Don says, "As a football fan, I know that that is by far the toughest position on the football team, because you have to catch the football while ten or eleven other guys are bearing down on you, all ready to kill you, and you have no one else with you." Dad pipes in, "And I only weighed one hundred and thirty-five pounds at the time. I played both offence and defence against players that were two hundred and fifty to three hundred pounds. When I think back, it was stupid!"

Once my parents married and started having children, they bought their first house in Copeland Park. It was a new community with many baby boom children. Volunteers in the community were in demand. My father decided to volunteer to be in charge of recreation. At that time, there was no municipal parks and recreation department. He had to scrounge to arrange for the development of the first local park, which no longer exists. It was eventually displaced by a townhouse development off Craig Henry Drive. But in the 1950s and early 1960s, my father was able to create a park with swings, a baseball diamond, and hockey rink. He says, "The Kiwanis Club donated the boards for the rink. There was a small recreation committee that I could call upon to help me with tasks, such as putting up the rink boards. I also had an arrangement with the fire department. I had to telephone them when the rink needed watering. They would send around a fire truck. They would then hook up a hose to the nearest fire hydrant." A little later on, my father also arranged for a rink in the small park near the corner of Navaho Drive and Erindale Drive. This was the rink closest to our home. My brothers and I would literally spend every moment we weren't in school or having dinner skating on this rink. At one point, we lived beside it. When it was time to come home in the evening, my parents would flash the lights in their bedroom as the signal ... and you couldn't say you didn't see it! Although at the start my father was responsible for ongoing maintenance of this rink as well, eventually, it was taken over by the City of Ottawa.

My father also loved coaching. He coached house league hockey in Copeland Park. His big claim to fame was initiating the careers of two future National Hockey League players. The first team he coached was the team my oldest brother, Don, played on. At that time, my father was approached by Doug Wilson Senior, one of the people responsible for recreation in Bel Air Heights, the adjoining community. Wilson told my father that his son, Doug Wilson Junior, was playing as a goalkeeper on one of their teams. He said, "I don't want my son to play in goal. He doesn't want to play in goal. Is there a chance that you would put him on your team?" Ever the positive guy, my father's immediate rely was, "Sure, bring him around." Doug Jr. was younger than Don, and he wasn't very big at the time. But he joined the team and my father found him to be a steady player. Other than Don, Doug Jr. was the best player on the team. My father put him on defence. They won the championship that year. Of course, as everyone knows, he ended up playing defence for the Ottawa 67s, Ottawa's junior team for the Ontario Hockey Association and then eventually the National Hockey League for the Chicago Black Hawks and the San Jose Sharks. Now, he is the General Manager for the San Jose Sharks.

The following year, Don moved up to another league and my middle brother, Steve, started to play. The two best players on the team that year were Steve and Bobby Smith; they also won the championship. My father remembers that they played their final game of the championship in the Auditorium, which used to be located downtown, where the YMCA is now. It was a big deal at that time to play there. Bobby Smith also ended up playing for the Ottawa 67s and then the NHL for the Montreal Canadiens and the Minnesota North Stars. He now owns a junior team in Nova Scotia, the Halifax Mooseheads.

Like my father, Don's first love was hockey. He recently found an old newspaper article in his wallet. The headline read that he had scored fourteen goals in three games. It seems unbelievable to him now that he could have scored that many goals. Don goes on to say, "I have learned that people like me, who were born in January, have a distinct advantage over people born in the latter part of the year. Most of my teammates did not have my advantage. Doug Wilson was two to three years younger than anyone else on the team, so he was at an even greater disadvantage. Doug was just a little tyke, so the fact that he was one of the top players on the team was a good indication of his talent. He went on to become a Norris Trophy winner, which is the best defenseman in the NHL, so this was certainly proven."

Dad comments, "Don did have a chance to play Junior B hockey and was keen on playing. It would have meant travelling all over Ontario and missing a lot of school." Don recalls, "Dad told me, I don't think you are ever going to be an NHL player and I think playing Junior B would be taking the wrong track in your life." Dad agrees, "I just said, no, I won't support you doing this." Dad remembers Don being very disappointed at the time: "He really put a lot of pressure on me. I felt like a real shit." Don says that he doesn't remember thinking ill of Dad for this decision. "In retrospect, it was a good thing," Don tells Dad.

One of my Dad's favourite pastimes is fishing. He developed this love of fishing from his own father. My grandfather never owned a car, so their fishing expeditions were limited to the distance they could travel on foot or by bicycle. Their favourite place to fish was in the Rideau River, between the railway bridge near what is now Carleton University and Hog's Back Falls. My father vividly remembers one particular fishing trip with his father and older brother Ernie. "On our way back home, we were starting to walk across the river along the railway bridge. We encountered a huge dog on the tracks. He was vicious. So we cut to the right going home, through the dump and into Ottawa South. My brother complained the whole walk home. Ernie stated, 'I'm never going fishing with you people again. That was terrible!' And he never did." My father on the other hand, was not bothered at all by the experience.

My brother Steve's fondest memories are of the many cottages my parents rented or owned. "The Glen Isle cottage on the Mississippi River, between Carleton Place and Almonte, was the cottage I most remember. Fishing was my favourite thing to do. I did a lot of it. The family did a lot of it together," he says. My youngest brother, Paul, agrees. "I love fishing. I haven't done it in a long time, but I used to spend my entire summer holidays and many weekends fishing at the cottage. I would fish anytime and anywhere. I enjoyed fishing whether I caught something or not. In contrast, Dad had his fishing down to a science. Dad's favourite time to fish was in the evening. The prize for him was catching a pickerel. He had a precise area where he liked to fish. His method of choice was trolling using one of his five million professional lures. He was usually pretty successful." Clearly, my father passed his love of fishing on to the next generation.

When my parents bought their first cottage on Glen Isle in 1972, they also bought a family membership at the nearby Mississippi Golf Course. I have strong memories of the first time we played. At that time, you did not book tee times. Instead, each foursome wanting to play put a ball in a metal pipe trough at the first tee. When your ball rolled to the bottom of the trough, it was your turn to tee off. The down side of this was that you ended up with a crowd of people standing around the first tee. My father had played a few times, but the rest of us were complete novices. We were freaking out. My father got us together and said, "Take a look at the other golfers. Most of them are no better than you." We started to pay more attention, and sure enough, they were almost all putting their first ball in the creek or into the rough. It calmed us all right down. After that, we played every weekend. Much to the annoyance of my brothers and me, it was usually at an ungodly hour in the morning. Even at eighty-four, my father still played golf several times a week. At eighty-six, he still plays frequently, and as ever, he is typically the first player on the golf course. He is renowned for playing rain or shine.

After reading through my father's diaries from 1973 to 1996, I tease him, "I cannot believe the amount of notes you have made in every single diary about your golf grip. Every single one has copious, detailed notes on the front and back covers, at the top and bottom of many dated pages. It's unbelievable!" Both my mother and father immediately laugh. My mother states, "He is constantly changing it. I can hear him practicing in the basement, even now." I say, "I have never seen the like of it; pages and pages." Dad laughs, embarrassed. "It's always been a thing with me, my golf grip. I change it all the time. I put down little reminder notes." I comment, "But some of the entries are two pages long!" "Yeah. Yeah, that's right," he says. "As I opened each diary, I could not believe there was more." "I'm still making notes," he says.

Unlike the parents of most of our friends, our parents bought and sold many homes, cottages, and rural properties. One of the first properties they bought was a hundred-acre hobby farm located near Frankton, Ontario. My mother recalls that they bought the farm in 1970, just after the family fieldtrip to Banff, and just before they bought their first cottage. She says, "We bought it in the dead of winter. People thought we were crazy buying a rural property in the winter." But my father could identify the vegetation popping up through the snow and knew by the type of species what the property was like. Dad says with great fondness, "I remember going to the farm during the winter and cross-country skiing into the back of the property. It was beautiful." This property was a real introduction to rural living. As a family, we cleaned out the barn, re-tinned the barn roof, and cultivated and weeded a big vegetable garden throughout the summer only to find the neighbour's cows had gotten in and eaten everything just as the produce was ready to harvest. We fought an out-of-control grass fire, dragged wood rails into place so that the fencing could be redone to prevent the cows from getting into the property, and, most worrisome of all, avoided hunters' bullets in the fall. It was hard, sweaty work. It probably cured my brothers and me from ever wanting to own a hobby farm.

My father actually liked the property enough to want to build a house there. However, in the end, they only owned it a couple of years. My mother comments, "You were all teenagers at the time and you were bugging us to buy a property on the water." Yeah! On the water and without all the hard work! This is when my parents decided to buy their first cottage. It was located on Glen Isle, a small island on the Mississippi River between Carleton Place and Almonte. The cottage's picturesque location was teeming with frogs, fish, and water snakes. The narrow channel and back channel, rapids and pools, provided endless hours of discovery and entertainment. "We sold the cottage on Glen Isle because we had been having a lot of trouble with kids breaking in," my father says. It wasn't really a cottage area. Most of the people lived there year-round but there was no one they knew well enough to ask to keep an eye on the cottage when they weren't there. It was when they were in this frame of mind that my parents saw another cottage on Mississippi Lake and decided to buy it. They sold one cottage and bought the next one the same week. "1980 was a good time to sell," they both say.

After my mother's stroke in 1995, they sold the Mississippi Lake cottage. It was probably the least accessible cottage they could have owned, with a high, steep, rocky shoreline. Not long after that, my parents also sold their trailer in Titusville, Florida. My father says, "I wasn't sorry to get rid of both of them. I had my hands full looking after Marg." My mother agrees with this sentiment. "It wasn't a great time to sell, but I was at St. Vincent's Hospital undergoing rehabilitation. It was not a memorable time of my life."

Of all the properties my parents have owned, the one my father is sorry they sold was twenty acres of mature white pine located near Middleville, Ontario. They advertised the property and one of the people who responded said he was an outdoor guy interested in the big pines. Well this spoke to my father's own love for the property, so they sold it to him. But, my father scornfully states, "The bloody guy subdivided the property and cut down all the big pines. He ruined the property doing it." In hindsight he says, "We didn't really need the money at that time. We never wanted to build on it. It was just a beautiful property to walk through. It had lots of snowshoe rabbits and deer, and of course, these immense white pines. It bothers me that all those trees were cut down."

Even at age eighty-four, a few weeks after selling their home of thirty years to move into a retirement residence, my father was musing about buying another property. Old habits die hard.

Going to country auctions was another favourite pastime for both of my parents. They starting going to auctions after they bought the Glen Isle cottage. Some nice pieces of old furniture were left in the cottage when they bought it. This was the first experience we had in refinishing furniture. My parents got the antique bug and started going to local auctions. Through a subscription to the Carleton Place newspaper, they were able to find out about upcoming auctions and planned their weekends accordingly. Often they golfed early and then would go to an auction afterwards. They soon became a fan of auctioneer Howard McNeely. My father comments, "It reached the stage where we knew a lot of the regulars. Howard knew us. We knew who all the dealers were." They furnished the entire cottage with their auction purchases. "We got a lot of good things," my mother says.

Funnily enough when I ask my father what his favourite acquisition was, he instead reminisces about the one that got away. His biggest regret is not getting an all-pine cupboard with a complex network of compartments. My mother agrees, "It was a really nice piece." My father remembers, "I was bidding it up, when someone whispered to me, 'You're bidding against the family. You're not going to get that.'" It was an estate sale. A number of family members wanted it. He realized he was competing against people with a strong emotional tie to the piece, so he backed off. But, he laments, "It was really nice!"

My father managed to accumulate quite a collection of old postcards and photographs. My mother could never pass up blue china. My father says, "Any china that had blue in it, Margaret would bid on it." My mother agrees. In particular, she remembers a blue and white washstand set, pitcher, and bowl. Another item that stands out for her was a large colourful rug that used to grace their dining room. "I loved that rug. It was my birthday present one year. Gerry paid more than we normally would have for it. I think it was three hundred dollars at the time. It was a really nice rug," she says. There is nothing like the thrill of bidding on something special, and getting it!

21
IN-LAWS, NOT A DIRTY WORD

Growing up, I never understood when comedians made jokes about their in-laws. Neither of my sets of grandparents interfered negatively in our family dynamics. Both relationships were always positive and genial.

My father's parents, Wilfred and Brigitte (Hill) Mulligan lived in Ottawa. We used to visit them every Sunday after church. They were an integral part of our weekly routine. On the other hand, my mother's parents, Donald and Loretta (Parisien) McDonald, lived in Montreal when we were young, later retiring back to Cornwall, near where they were both born and raised. While we often visited them in Montreal, the place we spent the most time with my maternal grandparents was at their cottage on the St. Lawrence River.

In 1944, Grampa McDonald bought a lot on Penville Bay, part of a widening of the St. Lawrence River called Lake St. Francis. The closest village is Rivière Beaudette. Mr. Groulx, a farmer, owned all the surrounding lands. His home was located right on Highway 2. A sign in front of his house read "Worm for sale." It was once featured in *Maclean's* magazine, speculating on whether Mr. Groulx had managed to sell his worm yet!

When I ask my mother whether my grandmother liked going to the cottage in the early years, she responds with an emphatic "No! She was not keen to start with." Apparently, this was vintage behaviour for my grandfather. My mother says, "When Dad bought our house on Rosselyn Avenue, my mother had never even seen it. She cried and cried and cried when we moved in because it was in such bad shape. My father just carried on." That's what happens when you are married to a stoic engineer. In his defence, my grandfather could see its potential. Once it was renovated, it was an elegant duplex located in the very desirable Montreal neighbourhood of Westmount. I have fond memories of that house: the wide dramatic central staircase, the narrow creaky back staircase to the kitchen, and the hourly bong of the mantelpiece clock in my grandfather's den. This was particularly useful when we visited for Christmas. I recall lying in bed for hours and hours listening for the right number of bongs for the hour my parents said we could get up and check what Santa had brought us.

My grandfather became interested in a cottage when some of his colleagues at Bell Telephone initiated the idea. In the end a group of four or five bought cottage properties in the same area. A year later, my grandfather had a cottage built on the property based on his own design. My mother recalls, "The initial cottage was a simple box. It was very rough; nothing was finished. When you entered the cottage, it was directly into a living room, dining room, and kitchen." There were two bedrooms in the rear of the cottage. Early on, there was no indoor bathroom. "We had an outhouse for quite a few years," my mother says. They also didn't have the money right away to finish the cottage on the inside.

A later addition included a much-desired indoor bathroom. It also included an extension to the living room and a second storey loft the full length of the cottage. This is where my mother and her two younger sisters slept. Her only brother, George, the youngest, slept in the other downstairs bedroom.

The knotty pine panelling I remember so vividly as a child was also added to finish the inside walls and ceiling of the cottage. I loved the knotty pine. I recall lying in bed in the upstairs loft and staring at the ceiling looking for whimsical shapes in the knots. What my father remembers most was lying in bed upstairs, hearing the lapping of waves on the shore. "I found it very soothing," he says.

In the early days, my grandparents didn't have a car. My grandfather would rent a car, for one day in the spring and one day in the fall, to take the family to and from the cottage for the summer. During the week, he would take a bus that travelled along Highway 2 from Montreal. It would drop him off at a store on the highway. My mother recalls that the family habitually used to walk up to meet him.

How did they get food without a car? My mother says they were lucky, an iceman came around to the cottages every day during the week, a bread man once a week, and a fruit and vegetable man a couple of times a week. "There was not a lot of selection. That's what my mother didn't like. It was hard to get fresh produce. There was even a guy from Rivière Beaudette who carried meat. Mother used to speak French with him." It was one of the few times my mother remembers her mother speaking French, her first language. This interaction was a weekly highlight for my grandmother.

My grandparents had a heavy mahogany boat at the cottage. It took a whole gang of people to put it in and take it out of the water every year. It also had to be painted annually and was stored in a shed over the winter. My father remembers them taking the boat across the St. Lawrence a couple of times. He says, "It was a long way with a little motor. You could only do it on rare calm days." As a teenager, my mother used to plead with her father to buy a nicer boat. It never worked. She says, "You know my father, he never said no, he just didn't say anything."

When my parents were first married, with young kids, they couldn't afford a cottage or summer vacations. My grandparents' cottage became a frequent summer destination. My father recalls, "Your grandparents always welcomed us. They even arranged for us to have the cottage to ourselves every summer for one week in June, before I left on a fieldtrip." My grandparents would come up on the weekends. I remember this being a big part of my childhood, playing badminton and croquet, fishing, and sitting in the big willow over the river with my legs dangling out over the water.

My oldest brother, Don, has similar fond memories. "I remember spending hours and hours collecting raspberries and strawberries. For some reason, I liked to do that. I only ever remember getting a brief warning, "If a stranger comes up to you and wants you to get in their car, don't go."

My father comments, "In hindsight, one of the advantages you had as children was that you had to improvise a lot, because there just weren't a lot toys and certainly no electronics to play with. You had to make up your own fun. Many kids wouldn't have done the things you did. You were creative." A testament to this is a famous family photo of Don playing with rocks in the parking lot behind a townhouse my parents once rented on Kingston Avenue. We may have been creative, but we also weren't constrained like many of our friends. We were allowed a lot of freedom. Every chance we got, we took off into the woods to build forts, to collect snakes, or to explore an old quarry.

Don chuckles and says, "The only dastardly thing I have ever known our father to have done is to cut down a neighbour's tree." Now before you rush to judgment, I need to provide a little background. Our grandparents' cottage property had several white poplars. This nuisance tree is weak-wooded and therefore susceptible to breakage. They also aggressively spread by underground root suckers. Basically, not a tree you want planted anywhere on or near your property. Both Don and Dad clearly recall the hell they went through in helping Grampa McDonald to remove two of these trees from the cottage property. Don fervently states, "I will never forget those trees! I remember digging and digging and digging. It was as if we were digging to China. You would finally dig out a root and think that was it, and then you would dig a little deeper and there was another root. It just went on and on. The hole was so big you could hardly see my head." Even after we removed the trees, there were still roots that were missed, and they continued to sucker for years afterward. When you played badminton or croquet on the lawn in bare feet, it was painful to step on one of these coarse suckers. Don reiterates, "I hated those trees!"

You will therefore understand the reaction a few years later when one of our neighbours on Erindale Drive planted a white poplar in their back yard, close to the property line. Don vividly remembers walking out toward the back gate and finding his father sprawled out on his stomach on the ground in the neighbour's yard. He had his pruning shears extended as far as he could reach on the verge of making a cut when Don quietly crept up to the fence and said, "Dad, what are you doing?" Don says that even though Dad was lying flat on the ground, his whole body rose up about two feet in the air. "I'm sure his heart was pumping right through his chest." Dad confirms this, "It was. As I was about to cut it, I was feeling guilty." Dad says, "I thought, he's planted this bloody tree and it's going to spread all over my property. I was doing him a favour. Only later did I find out that he got the tree from his mother. Even so, I was saving him from himself. I could not believe when he planted it, and he was so proud of it." "It was so out of character for him," Don says, "But in light of what we had been through with the trees at the cottage, I totally understood."

My brother, Steve, also has many memories of Granny and Grampa's cottage. He too singles out the cutting of the infamous white poplars. He especially remembers the big hole

184

we dug in the front lawn. "We just kept digging and digging and digging." It is telling that both Steve and Don repeat digging three times each in separate accounts of the event.

My grandparents sold the cottage in 1972. At this point, my mother begins to recount a story that is complete news to my father. "My father called and asked if we wanted the cottage. He said it was too much work for them now. He wanted to give it to us," likely because of all the families, ours visited the most. Of course, we were the only family living near it. My mother told my grandfather, "No, we are in the process of buying a cottage ourselves and it is a little far to drive." At this point, my mother realizes what she has said, and turns to my father admitting, "I never consulted you." My father is amazed, "I never even knew about it until now. It wasn't that far. I would have jumped at the chance, but obviously you weren't interested." Upon reflecting on it for a few minutes, my father follows up with, "In hindsight, as I think about it, it is probably just as well, because if we had have either been gifted it or bought it from your parents, the other siblings might have been upset." My mother immediately agrees, "You're right!" "That's probably why Marg didn't want to get involved in it. It was probably the right decision," my father says.

My maternal grandfather, Donald J. McDonald was born and raised on a farm near Glen Nevis, not far from Alexandria, Ontario. He was a proud electrical engineer graduating from Queen's University in Kingston, Ontario, in 1926. He was employed by Bell Telephone, at their headquarters in Montreal, his entire working life. A more dedicated and loyal employee would be difficult to find. My mother says, "When my father first joined Bell, they sent him to Schenectady, New York. I have a picture of him up a telephone pole." That was just to start him off. By the time my parents got married, he was working at the new Bell Telephone Company of Canada building at Beaver Hall. My mother goes on to say, "When I was young, we would often go up to the big lookout on Mount

Royal. Three large buildings, Bell Telephone, Sun Life Assurance, and Royal Bank, stood out from all the others in downtown Montreal." My mother also remembers, "When I was in high school, I used to see my father drive by during the day. He was working on telephones in cars. This was a new technology then." This would have been in the mid-1940s.

One of my grandfather's career highlights was working as transmission engineer for the Mid-Canada Line, a line of radar stations located across the middle of Canada. It acted as an early warning system against concerns about a possible Soviet attack on North America. Such stations would transmit microwaves that would bounce off any object in their path. In a 1987 letter to my uncle, George McDonald, my grandfather wrote, "I had worked on the first microwave projects in Ontario and Quebec, but from June 1953 to July 1957 I was in the Special Contract Department working on Defence Projects. It was in this period that the system was extended from Toronto to Victoria, British Columbia. The most spectacular part was building stations through the mountains from Calgary to Vancouver because of the rugged nature of the country and the daunting physical problems of construction at such sites." These National Defence stations were only in operation for a short time from the late 1950s to mid-1960s. The northern Distant Early Warning (DEW) Line then took over as the main early warning system for North America.

My mother recalls, "My father studied almost every night in his den. He taught himself all about satellites. We were strictly forbidden from disturbing him during this time. Because of this effort, towards the end of his career, my father was loaned to Bell Northern Research where he started to work on satellite communications. My mother and father went to meetings in Oslo, Norway, on satellite research. He retired soon afterwards, in 1966. I think he realized the effort required to keep up was more than he was willing to commit to at that point in his career." According to my grandfather's records, he still consulted for a year after he retired on a Communication Satellite System for Canada. Uncle George sent me a copy of a company newsletter, *Bell News*, dated March 13, 1963. The front-page story was *Five Bell engineers take part in Geneva satellite talks.*

> *Five Bell engineers have played a major role in an historic international conference at Geneva preparing the way for world-wide satellite communications.*
>
> *Attending their first Plenary Conference of the International Radio Consultative Committee as members of a six-man delegation of The Telephone Association of Canada, the Engineers were prominent in hammering out the ground rules defining functions and limits of both satellite communications and existing radio relay systems in order to assure their harmonious co-existence.*
>
> *The recommendations drawn up at the conference will provide the background and guidelines for October's Extraordinary Administrative Radio Conference — a convention at which all governments in the United Nations will negotiate international agreements on satellite communications.*
>
> *Representing the Telephone Association of Canada were C.H. McGuire, General Engineering, Transmission, Headquarters; J.W. Wilson, Staff Engineer, Headquarters; D.J. McDonald, Area Radio Engineer, Toll Area; D.M. Hinton, Supervising Engineer, Headquarters; L.G. Buck, General Staff Engineer, Headquarters; and B.R. Tupper, Assistant Vic-President, British Columbia Telephone Company.*
>
> *Delegations from 75 nations followed three weeks of intensive give-and-take in study groups by finally reaching agreement on a lengthy roster of recommendations at the 10-day plenary assembly in the Bâtiment Électorale in Geneva. The delegations were divided roughly into two factions — those advancing the aims and designs of satellite communications and those protecting the functions of radio relay systems.*

My grandfather once told me about advice he had given to my

mother's youngest sister, Katherine, just prior to her marriage to a civil engineer interested in major infrastructure projects. As an engineer himself, my grandfather knew that this would mean they would have to travel to major project sites across Canada and around the world. He asked my aunt if she was prepared to do this. Clearly she was, and they did in fact do exactly as my grandfather predicted. I figured he must have done something similar to my mother, so I asked her. At this point, my father perks up with interest. "I'd really like to hear this!" He was completely unaware this had happened. The talk happened during the year my mother was a dietetic intern in Toronto. My grandfather was in Toronto for business when he asked my mother to meet him at his hotel. He inquired what her plans were with respect to my father. "I told him that I thought that I was going to marry him," she says. What he really wanted to know was whether she felt certain this was the right thing for her. She assured him that it was. It seems to have worked out pretty well since they have been married for sixty years and counting.

22
DECISION TO RETIRE

My father liked his job, but what made him first think about retiring was the experience of downsizing the public service in the mid-1980s. The Assistant Deputy Minister, Ed LeRoux, called a meeting of senior managers to announce that they had to downsize by ten percent. My father says, "As a manager, if they were going to downsize, I was willing to downsize my Institute. I knew this was my job. I could come up with people." But LeRoux said, "Oh, no, no, we'll tell you who to downsize." LeRoux wanted to downsize some good people and keep poor performers who my father would have gotten rid of. The people who had curried LeRoux's favour by doing his bidding were safe; those who had just focused on doing their jobs were not. "Some managers were willing to do this to preserve their career ambitions. I never felt that my job as Director was something that I wanted to hang onto at all cost. I knew I could retire and quite happily become an Honorary Research Associate," he says. He had over thirty-five years of service. He was only staying because he had enjoyed his job. He decided to retire. This was in 1987.

My father's Executive Secretary, Rosanna (Menchini) Carson, says that she could see his retirement coming. She says, "In the last year, he would attend meetings and come back so frustrated and angry. A lot of the time, he wouldn't tell me why, but he would not be in a good mood. I knew they wanted to reorganize, but I didn't know the details." Carson remembers that towards the end of his tenure as Director, my father told her that he was being made to retire. "He would come back from meetings very frustrated. He told me that they were pushing him out." When I declare surprise at this, she says, "Unless he was just telling me that because he wanted to retire and he knew I would be upset if he did." She also adds, "He told me, I don't agree with them."

My father is emphatic in stating, "Nobody pushed me out! I retired primarily because I was told there were cuts coming, staff would have to be laid off, but senior management in the Sir John Carling Building would be making the decisions. They would tell me which areas of my Institute were no longer a priority and which staff would be laid off. I felt that they did not know what they were talking about. I was in the best position to make those decisions. As a matter of fact, at the time, I said to Marg that if I was allowed to cut ten percent of staff and was given leeway to do it as I saw fit, the Institute would probably benefit from getting rid of people that were a drain on its resources. But to cut ten percent mindlessly across the board would undoubtedly get rid of some good people. I just didn't feel it was right. It was not something that I wanted to be part of, so I decided to retire."

When my father finally decided on a specific date of retirement, the first person at work that he told was Ian Smith. Smith, an entomologist, had been my father's Assistant Director for years. My father comments, "I felt he would be a good Director. He was a good scientist. I thought that it would be important to continue to have a scientist as Director of the Institute." My father visited Smith in his lab to inform him of his decision to retire and when. "He was shocked," my father says. My father further shocked Smith by telling him, "I would like to know

190

whether or not you are interested in being Director of this Institute. You have a good background, better than anyone else. I think you would make a good Director." Smith was taken aback. His response was that he was going to have to think about it. My father told him, "Well, I want to formally announce my retirement soon, so I would like to know your decision by tomorrow."

The next day, Smith came to my father and told him, "I talked it over with my wife. I am interested in my area of mites. I don't think that I would want to become a full-time manager. I would not want to go through all the things I see you going through. I don't want you to recommend me to be Acting Director." As soon as he left, my father proceeded immediately to the Director General's office to inform Ed LeRoux of his decision to retire. This announcement left the door open for Robert Trottier, who had been lobbying hard for some time for a job as Director of one of the Institutes.

☒ January 18, 1986 – I had a hard time sleeping last night because of the poor treatment that I am getting from Halstead and LeRoux.

☒ February 28, 1986 – I am really fed up with my job and doubt that I will last another year.

☒ June 3, 1986 – I went to my last Director's Meeting. LeRoux was wishy washy as usual. It was comforting that all of the Directors are experiencing the problems associated with downsizing.

Some staff were surprised when my father announced his retirement. Others were not. There was a lot of gossip and speculation going around the Institute in those days. Carson tells me, "Some probably even thought, oh good, now I can get away with what I want to do. Little did they realize what was coming next!" Trottier did succeed my father as Director. My father feels he was chosen not only because he was an entomologist and a francophone, but most importantly because

LeRoux probably wanted to stop Trottier from bugging him for a director position. "He turned out to be a disaster. It is too bad Ian Smith didn't take the job," my father says with regret. In any case, Trottier did not last long as Director.

- September 29, 1986 – I met with Halstead and the other Directors. Things look poor for the future and I do not envy future managers. The Directors were surprised at my retirement but seemed to envy me. I had quite a few of our staff express concern at my retirement.

- October 3, 1986 – Several people came to offer their regrets. Rosanna will have fun with Trottier.

It turned out that just after my father announced his retirement, Ed LeRoux retired. Ron Halstead, who was Director General, became Acting Deputy Minister and my father became Acting Director General until he retired.

- October 20, 1986 – I received my letter from LeRoux – fully satisfactory and 1% (bonus). My support of biosystematics has cost me lots of money. I am really worked up about Halstead's appraisal and have decided to resign as Acting Director General tomorrow.

- October 21, 1986 – I did not resign as A/DG but cancelled my trip to Brandon. I expressed my displeasure on my fully satisfactory to Halstead and he stated that it was not his fault.

- November 20, 1986 - I wrote a letter to Halstead regarding my appraisal and snooty comments on my document. I did not sign it.

- November 25, 1986 – To see Halstead at 8 am and he disclaimed all responsibility for my rating. He confirmed that Ian de la Roche has asked for permission to dump the mum show.

- November 27, 1986 – Trottier is going around saying that things will improve considerably with BRI under him.

- January 13, 1987 – One month until my retirement do. I am finding it harder to get up in the morning.

✍ January 23, 1987 – I have been down lately because of how I left my managers job. I should not let Halstead's poor management spoil my 8 years of overall satisfaction as a research manager. Perhaps I am also worrying about my future finances and what I will do with myself.

✍ February 11, 1987 – I hear negative vibes about my regime from the entomologists. It sure is discouraging to hear the yahoos blaming all their troubles on me. I'm glad that I stepped down.

My father had no real regrets about retiring. He did not want to stay during the downsizing. He does not recall if the terminations senior management wanted were done. Once he decided to retire, he made a specific decision not to get involved. He didn't even want to talk about it with anyone. Any staff that would come to him wanting to discuss it, he would tell them, "That's it. I'm not a manager any more. I'm retiring and I don't want to have anything to do with it." Even after he retired and became an Honorary Research Associate, he continued with this approach.

My father's concerns for how Carson would fare working for Trottier turned out to be well founded. When I asked Carson to compare the three Directors she worked with, she says, "Oh, there isn't even a comparison. Dr. Trottier was the worst director I ever worked for."

Apparently during his tenure, Trottier was rarely around when staff needed to see him. Carson states, "He would typically saunter in late every single day at ten o'clock. He would leave for lunch and not return until three o'clock in the afternoon." Aside from the obvious, this caused big problems for Carson. She would arrive at seven o'clock each day so that she could leave by three-thirty in the afternoon. She says, "I was a single mother. I had to go home. My son was just a little boy at that time. On a regular basis, just as I was getting ready to leave, he would call me into his office and want me to take dictation for letters for him. He just laughed at the predicament he caused me." She says that it was like this day after day. She would have to do a lot of his work. Because his English was poor, she had to write his letters. She ended up bringing work home to finish these letters and other correspondence. She says that he gave her more and more responsibility. When she left, two people were hired to do the work she had been doing. "It was just too much," she says.

Two weeks after she quit in 1990, she submitted her resume to the Nepean Police Department. She was hired over the phone. She says that it was such a joy to be happy again at work. She worked steadily after she left and just recently retired.

Trottier left the Institute a year after Carson. She says, "I met him a few years later in an antique shop on Bank Street. He recognized me. He was with his wife." He yelled, "Rosanna, Rosanna!" Carson says, "He used to tell me how much all his former secretaries loved him. I took one look at him and lost it. I guess all the rage that I never had a chance to express to him for all the abuse I took from him for three years came out. I screamed, 'I hate you. Get away from me!' My husband was so embarrassed. His wife was just horrified. I yelled, 'This secretary will never miss you!' and walked out of the store."

Getting back to talking about her previous boss, Carson says, "Your father and I still exchange Christmas cards. He was a big part of my life for ten years. I felt like he was part of my family. My boss cared about me. I was twenty-two when I first started working at Agriculture Canada. Dave Hardwick had had a long-time secretary who had left to stay home with her children. He had really liked her. I was her replacement. I only worked for him for a short time before he retired. We were never close. When your father took over the position, he took me under his wing and we worked well together. It was kind of nice doing battle together," Carson says.

Her final words in the interview were these: "I truly cared for Mr. M. and still do. The years I worked with him were a good time in my life." As Carson pauses, overcome by emotion, she apologizes and then says, "We certainly had our ups and downs, you do when you see each other every day. But I loved my job. I absolutely loved working for your father."

23
HONORARY RESEARCH ASSOCIATE

At Agriculture Canada, about twenty-five percent of retiring scientists go on to become Honorary Research Associates. My father is one of them. "Most of the scientists that have opted to stay on as Research Associates tended to be the better scientists, the more dedicated and successful scientists. It's interesting," my father says, "some of the scientists just kept on as if they were full-time staff members. For other scientists, the day they retired, you never saw them again." Typically, there is an initial wave of those who keep on doing research for about four or five years. These scientists primarily use it as a transition to retirement. It enables them to finish outstanding research they are working on.

An Honorary Research Associate is similar to an emeritus professor at a university. It represents the ability for a scientist to keep doing research and having the work published. Honorary Research Associates are not paid anything beyond their generous public service pensions. At Agriculture Canada, they are provided with a place to work and the equipment and resources they need to carry out and publish their research. The Research Associate is attached to a regular staff member. If he or she needs resources, the request is made through the assigned staff person. My father has consistently worked as an Honorary Research Associate for over twenty-five years. There are similar retirement research programs elsewhere. My mother has a physiotherapist whose father is a physicist at the National Research Council. He is also able to continue to do research in his retirement years.

Not all scientists want to become Honorary Research Associates, and it is not automatic that those who do are approved to do so. Retiring scientists are required to make a written application for acceptance. If you are accepted, you are appointed for only one year. Thereafter, you apply and are reviewed on a yearly basis. You have to demonstrate your value and productivity to the Institute on an ongoing basis.

As an Honorary Research Associate, being a former Director presented its own unique set of challenges. When my father retired and first returned in the new role, staff kept approaching him for help in dealing with the new Director. "I made up my mind when I retired that I was not going to get involved in any problems or intrigue in the Institute," he says. For a least a year and a half, people would come to him and try to get him to intercede for them. My father flatly refused. He had had his own experience in dealing with a former Director who frequently tried to interfere with decisions on behalf of some of the scientists. My father had refused to allow this to happen to him and he certainly was not going to inflict his opinions on another Director. He does say, however, "In the many years since I retired, I have seen a lot of things going on that I am not impressed with and that make me sad." People say to him, "How can you stand it?" But he long ago determined, "It's not my problem anymore."

The main attraction for a scientist in becoming an Honorary Research Associate is the ability to keep using a lifetime of knowledge. My father agrees, "I have been working on certain plant groups for over fifty years. Because of the breadth of my knowledge, I can see certain things that other people haven't seen. I enjoy working on plant groups that other people have studied and coming up with something new. Over the years, I have been able to shed new light on plant groups that have baffled plant taxonomists for decades and in some cases centuries. They are not stupendous scientific revelations, but significant nonetheless. Occasionally, research doesn't go well and you get discouraged. But in general, since I retired, I have worked fairly consistently." He goes on to say, "I still have many things that I would like to investigate. Often, I have to put them on the back burner for a while as I deal with personal issues." While my father agrees that the intellectual stimulation and full use of his knowledge are positive values of being an Honorary Research Associate, the main thing that drives him to keep doing research is the personal satisfaction of a job well done.

Initially, my father's post-retirement research focused on projects he had been working on before he became a manager. When he retired, he decided to finish them. He says, "While I did some research while I was a manager, I didn't have the time to do any major projects. After I retired, I did a major taxonomic treatment of *Arabis*. Very few people in Canada had done something like this and I did it after I retired." It was something he had started early in his career, but stopped because another scientist, Ted Mosquin, wanted to work on *Arabis*. Mosquin had spent two full years in the field collecting a lot of material, but then didn't do anything with it. Many of the annotated specimens were not in the herbarium, but were stored in filing cases. My father knew they were there, so he decided to use this material as part of a broader investigation of the genus *Arabis*. He credited Mosquin with the material he had collected. "I never heard from Mosquin after the paper was published, but I'm sure that he was aware of it." My father's diary entries give a very good account of the process and thought he goes through in arriving at a new plant key.

✍ October 27, 1989 – I finished a preliminary identification of the Calder *Arabis* and some other specimens and a preliminary key.

✍ November 27, 1989 - I worked on *Arabis* key on the dining room table.[6]

✍ April 18, 1990 – Annotated *Arabis alpina* and *A. caucasica* and inserted them in the key.

✍ April 23, 1990 – Annotated *A. canadensis*. I started *A. pendulocarpa*, which may be tougher than I expected.

✍ April 25, 1990 – Worked on *A. pendulocarpa – collinsii* and related taxa.

✍ May 2, 1990 – Worked on the *A. pendulocarpa* complex. I still have trouble in defining its limits.

✍ May 3, 1990 – I finally decided on the limits of *pendulocarpa*. I am not sure that the DOA[7] specimen is an isotype of *A. collinsii*.

✍ July 23, 1990 – I finished another version of the *Arabis* key.

✍ August 23, 1990 – I finished annotating *Arabis pendulocarpa*.

✍ September 24, 1990 – I seem to have resolved most of the problems in *Arabis lyrata* vs. *kamchatika*.

✍ September 26, 1990 – I worked and finished *lyrata–kamchatika* and started *hirsuta* (it may be more complicated than I thought).

✍ October 12, 1990 – I identified *drummondii* and *lyallii*

✍ November 6, 1990 – Jack Gillett showed up with an old copy of Rollins' *Arabis* monograph.

---

[6] He worked on this while he was recovering from surgery.

[7] DAO is the official designation of the Department of Agriculture Ottawa for their Vascular Plant Herbarium. The designation CAN denotes a specimen from the Canadian National Museum herbarium and GH the Great Herbarium of Harvard University. Every herbarium in the world has such an acronym for their specimens. This allows scientists to source plant material.

- November 14, 1990 – I finished identifying all *Arabis* except the problems encountered. I started the key.

- November 23, 1990 – I worked on locating place of type descriptions and type. I finished Rollins 1941 and started Hopkins 1937.

- December 10, 1990 – I worked on finding the descriptions for *Arabis* types.

- December 11, 1990 – I started to list *Arabis* types under different herbaria.

- December 19, 1990 – I wrote a letter regarding *Arabis* types for Paul Catling's signature and updated the curator's addresses.

- April 3, 1991 – Started working on the Notre Dame *Arabis* types.

- April 5, 1991 – I finished the Notre Dame types and other specimens, recorded the data and returned them to Fred.

- April 12, 1991 – I started on the types of the Smithsonian.

- April 17, 1991 – I worked on New York Botanic Garden *Arabis* types.

- April 23, 1991 – I lectotypified *A. sparsiflora* with the help of Bernard Baum.

- April 24, 1991 – I finished *A. sparsiflora* and started to finalize *microphylla – macounii* – new species with *holboelli* trichomes and semi-sparsiflora siliques.

- April 26, 1991 – I started on the *shortii* complex.

- May 2, 1991 – I worked on redoing the *Arabis* key. I brought some materials home and finished the key there after lunch.

- May 6, 1991 – I pasted up annotation slips for *Arabis*.

- July 22, 1991 – I worked on *Arabis*. I am thinking of drastically reworking my key.

⌀ July 26, 1991 – I started on *Arabis* key with the second split-off the siliques.[8]

⌀ October 18, 1991 – I started to put annotated DAO *Arabis* in order.

⌀ October 29, 1991 – Cody showed me Mosquin's collections and I put some in a case downstairs and some in my room. I also brought all U.S. *Arabis* to my room.

⌀ October 30, 1991 – I started to identify all of Mosquin's *Arabis* represented in Canada.

⌀ October 31, 1991 – I identified many Mosquin specimens, some collected with me, and Gillett and Taylor material.

⌀ November 1, 1991 – I continued on Mosquin *Arabis*. I discussed with Cody ditching the count labels where there was a mixture and where the Mosquin count agreed with his tentative name but had the wrong base number for the actual specimens.

⌀ November 4, 1991 – I worked on the Mosquin *Arabis* in the morning. I found that an *Arabis glabra* was counted as 2n about 21. Obviously a mix up in the material or a bad count.

⌀ November 5, 1991 – I worked on Mosquin's *Arabis*. It is surprising how much of his material was collected on the *Physaria-Arabis* trip.[9]

⌀ November 7, 1991 – I finished identifying Mosquin *Arabis* and started to record the chromosome data. I found a collection from the University of Alberta that was unidentified by Mosquin and was to be returned by 1963.

⌀ November 8, 1991 – I compiled data on chromosome observations from Mosquin *Arabis* specimens.

⌀ November 14, 1991 – I finished the Mosquin *Arabis* today and started taking my chromosome data from specimens, arranging to move the identified Mosquin unmounted material out of my room to be mounted and duplicates

---

[8] Siliques are elongated seed capsules.

[9] This was a fieldtrip he and Mosquin took together.

distributed, and getting ready to file Mosquin's mounted material (now identified) into the collection.

🖉 December 5, 1991 – I worked on cleaning up the key and list of taxa.

🖉 December 6, 1991 – I went to the Saunders and photocopied the *Arabis* key. I decided to see what *Arabis* occur in Florida.

🖉 December 10, 1991 – I worked on the U.S. species of *Arabis*.

🖉 November 20, 1991 – I finished identifying all DAO *Arabis*, including Calder and Mosquin collections, except *Arabis* material that only occurs in the U.S.

In late 1991 or early 1992, the *Arabis* manuscript would have been submitted to *Rhodora*, the journal of the New England Botanical Club, for publication. It is typical for the review of such scientific journals to take years.

🖉 October 3, 1994 – I received my *Arabis* manuscript back from *Rhodora* and at first look the Editors suggestions are impractical with my limited time and resources.

🖉 October 5, 1994 – I looked over the *Arabis* reviews and after talking to Paul Catling and being promised help doing scanner photos of *Arabis* hairs, I decided to revise my manuscript for the editor.

🖉 October 7, 1994 – I started to gather trichomes of *Arabis* for SEM (scanning electron microscope) photos.

🖉 October 12, 1994 – I finished selecting trichome samples for SEM work. I worked with Giselle mounting specimens on mounts for SEM photographs. We made an appointment for scanner photographs next Wednesday afternoon.

🖉 October 14, 1994 – I started to revise the *Arabis* manuscript utilizing the reviewers' comments.

🖉 October 20, 1994 – I worked on the SEM with Giselle Mitrow. We did about 12 samples of *Arabis* trichomes at x75 and x150 and decided to redo those done earlier because of focusing problems.

⚕ October 28, 1994 – With some experimenting arrived at 20km as the best setting for my SEM photographs. I therefore did everything a third time at this setting and skipped curling.

⚕ November 3, 1994 – Gisele told me that 2/3 of our SEM pictures were poor.

⚕ November 16, 1994 – I mounted the mock-up of the SEM photographs on three plates and arranged for Paul Catling to bring the material to Biographic.

⚕ December 2, 1994 – I finally received my *Arabis* trichome plates from Biographic.

⚕ May 20, 1995 – Paul Catling approved my page charges for the *Arabis* manuscript.

⚕ June 7, 1995 – I wrote a letter today to the editor of *Rhodora* requesting info on what happened to the *Arabis* manuscript.

⚕ June 14, 1995 – I phoned the Editor of *Rhodora* and he told me that my *Arabis* manuscript would be out in the next issue of that journal.

In about 2006, Dr. Ihsan Al-Shehbaz, a botanist working out of the Missouri Botanical Garden, took on the job of compiling a summary of knowledge on the genus *Draba* for *Flora of North America*. Al-Shehbaz is considered the world authority on the mustard family, primarily working with tropical and sub-tropical species. Naturally, he sought out my father to handle the species from Canada and Alaska. Al-Shehbaz is a doer and wanted the work done within a certain length of time. The problem for my father was that, at the time, he was ill and having a lot of trouble coping. That said, he still did a lot of work for Al-Shehbaz. "I went through the herbarium at the Farm, and took out all the specimens that were fairly routine, with a name on them. I did not select anything that was unusual or might be a new species." My father was one of the few people, potentially the only person, who could identify all the specimens for Al-Shehbaz. My father says, "I put together eight or nine big boxes of *Draba* specimens and sent them down to Missouri." My father was pleased to be involved in this research, but it was an additional stress when he was already struggling with ill health. At a certain point, he made the hard decision to step back, even though it bothered him, because he is a doer himself. It was a good decision for him. He experienced a great sense of relief once he did so. With the specimens my father and others sent him, Al-Shehbaz was able to complete his contribution for the publication *Flora of North America*.

In the last few years, my father has been feeling better. He was able to start looking at the unusual *Draba* specimens. As a result, he realized that about eight to ten species were missing from the *Draba* section of *Flora of North America*. In 2012, Al-Shehbaz approached him about working together on a more scientific treatment of the genus *Draba* in Canada, the United States, and Greenland. This work fills in the gaps, with a lot of new material on the more complicated species of *Draba* not covered in the *Flora of North America*. It contains descriptions, a revised plant key and publishes the names of seven new species. It is a summary of the accumulated knowledge on *Draba* within these geographic areas. This comprehensive paper was published in late 2013 in the *Harvard Papers in Botany* just shy of my father's eighty-sixth birthday.

My father comments, "There is a tendency for Honorary Research Associates to come in less and less as time goes on for various reasons, often due to declining health." In my father's case, my mother's stoke in 1995 changed everything. "When I became a caregiver, being an Honorary Research Associate became a lot more difficult," he says. There were periods, especially when my mother first came home from the hospital, when he was hardly doing any research. Even after things stabilized, my father never went in for more than the morning, usually for about three hours, because he didn't want to leave my mother alone for long periods. He says, "The trouble is that when you are working on a research project, you have to have some continuity. It is difficult if you can't get back to it for two weeks. I wouldn't have been able to keep doing research if I didn't have a computer at home. I probably do as much or more work at home, even now, than when I'm in my office in the Saunders Building. I'm continually sending files back and forth between my home and office. I do my microscope observations at the office, but a lot of the writing is done at home."

From my perspective, I would say that without any doubt my father's ability to keep doing research has been a huge contributing factor to his coping for so long in the very difficult role as my mother's primary caregiver. When I ask him if he agrees, my father pauses and then thoughtfully says, "That's a good question. I never thought about it. It probably does. It's an island away from the constant demands. I would like to be doing more research, but I can't. I enjoy the time when I can. It's pure pleasure." At various points over the years, as he completed a major research project, my father would contemplate giving it up, especially at times when the pressure of caregiving weighed heavily on him. Seeing the benefits it brought him, I was always a strong advocate for him continuing.

"About ten percent of retired scientists would stay in it for the long haul," my father says. Evert Lindquist, a world-renowned authority on mites, is an active Honorary Research Associate in his seventies. The recently deceased Bill Cody was active well into his eighties. Cody had been the curator of the plant herbarium while employed with the Institute. Once he retired, he continued to take care of the collection. Gradually, others started to take over the role. Paul Catling is the current curator. He phased in, as Bill Cody tapered out. The program also provides a great transition for the Institute. Stan Hughes, a famous mycologist, still comes into the Institute in his nineties.

My father comments, "He's not producing a lot anymore, but coming into the office allows him to keep in contact not only with his colleagues at the Institute, but also with the broader international scientific community. Most of the scientists who come in and stay on for a long time are those who have an international network of contacts built up over the years. Of course this network tends to decrease as people elsewhere retire or die off." These highly experienced scientists, with a lot of knowledge and contacts, are a very valuable resource still available to the Institute.

It is interesting that not as many of the more recently retired scientists are continuing their research. My father confirms that the ranks of Honorary Research Associates are currently dominated by the old guard, like himself. He has no idea why that is. I asked Stephen Darbyshire for his perspective on this trend. He comments, "I would say yes, that there are fewer Research Associates in the botany/entomology/mycology group now than before. Right now, about half the people in the mycology section are retired Honorary Research Associates. Your father is the only one in botany right now. My sense is that the reasons are complicated and perhaps driven partly by chance and partly by circumstances. One thing that has affected the numbers is that there is no longer a mandatory retirement age in the federal government, so people tend to be working longer. Being on staff gives a scientist more benefits and access to more resources than would be available to them as a Research Associate. There are currently two scientists in their seventies still on staff. They will never willingly retire because they don't have to and they have no other outside pursuits that interest them."

Darbyshire goes on to say, "Certainly anyone dependent on a well-funded lab will have difficulty staying on as an Honorary Research Associate, as it would be hard to get the cash flow established to maintain such a facility. This is partly the reason that Suzanne Warwick (who used DNA studies to distinguish between plant populations) did not become an Honorary Research Associate." Darbyshire says, "She would not have been able to continue the work she was doing simply because the money would not be available for expensive equipment. It's different for your father and his ilk who are content and productive with existing facilities, such as a microscope and use of the herbarium and other collections. It doesn't cost the department anything to keep them on, or at least nothing of significance."

Darbyshire's comments highlight two new conditions in the workplace. First, some employees, and especially scientists, are willing to take advantage of an extended mandatory retirement age and increasing incentives to stay in the workforce longer. In the case of scientists and researchers, this probably backfires, since historically the best and brightest of them were already willing to stay on, at no additional cost to the taxpayer. However, regarding the second condition, with the increased use of technology in all jobs, it is now difficult to impossible for many professions to continue on their own without major support. Not just the expensive equipment, but the frequent updating of equipment and the IT support that goes along with it makes it very difficult for many professions to operate under their own steam anymore.

A post-retirement program that allows highly productive knowledge workers to continue with their work in a more limited way is a great concept. It is probably best applied in association with a pension plan and to more solitary professions. It would not work as well with professions dependent on the involvement of a team of people. At a time when we are already experiencing a severe reduction of corporate knowledge, with a prediction that it is only going to get worse, many other organizations would do well to emulate this type of program. Such a program also offers a less structured, more fluid way for knowledge workers to stay in touch with their profession. It responds well to the ebb and flow of outside influences associated with aging. It also allows for the retention of corporate knowledge that current employees would not know about. My father says, "Frequently people wonder about certain events or actions from the past. They may have heard second- or third-hand information about something, but don't know the details. Often I am the only person still alive who can provide a first-hand account of what really happened and the reasons why." As a former manager, he was often involved in the actions or decisions. He also has a lot of knowledge about the work done by people who present staff never knew. Not only am I very proud of my father's ongoing contributions to science, but I also envy greatly the opportunity afforded to him and wish that more creative opportunities of a similar nature become more commonly available before my own retirement.

24
GOLDEN RETIREMENT YEARS

The nine years immediately after my father retired in 1987 were the golden years of his retirement, actually for both of my parents. They were healthy, active, and interested in a wide variety of things. Many activities they had been doing together before my father's retirement, but were now able to participate in more fully, such as golfing, gardening, cottage life in the summer, and travelling to Florida in the winter.

My father has always been an avid gardener. In fact, he comes from a long line of avid gardeners. He says, "I just like growing things." While he certainly took pleasure in everything he grew, his real pride and joy was always his vegetable garden. Ever the scientist, my father was always testing the seed of new vegetable cultivars and gardening methods. For twenty-eight years, my parents lived in Carleton Heights, an area bounded by Prince of Wales Drive, Meadowlands Drive, and Fisher Avenue. The large urban lots are ideal for gardening, except for the heavy clay soils and high water table. Over time, my father discovered a Chinese method of growing vegetables whereby you mound up rows of soil in which you grow the plants. Initially, he had done this because he was looking for a method that would not require yearly rototilling of the soil. With this method, you walk between the rows, thereby reducing soil compaction. However, the method also had an even more important benefit. It raised the plants out of the often water-logged clay soil.

My parents' rear yard spanned midway between two other properties, owned by equally avid gardeners, both elderly Italians who spoke almost no English. However, they were always curious as to what my father was up to in his garden and occasionally had brief communication, gardener-to-gardener, over the back hedge. After one particularly rainy summer, one of the Italians, Urbano, approached my father wanting to know why his garden had done so much better than his had. Within the limits of a common language, my father was able to explain his raised mound technique at least partially. He also brought Urbano down to the basement to see his seedlings and seed packets. Urbano and most of the other older Italian gardeners only used seed stock derived from traditional Italian cultivars they had brought over when they had immigrated to Canada. They carefully harvested and dried the seed they needed to produce the next year's crop. My father's gardening activities were a constant source of interest and amazement for these traditional Italian gardeners. They may not have spoken each other's language, but the language of gardening was well understood among them.

In 1972, my parents had purchased a cottage on a small island located in the Mississippi River, beside the Mississippi Golf Course, near Almonte. Shortly after buying the cottage, they signed the entire family up as members of the nearby golf course. Once we all moved away from home, my parents continued to play at the Mississippi Golf Course until 1991, when they switched to the Irish Hills Golf Course near Carp. It was much closer to Ottawa and they knew a lot more people who played at Irish Hills. They each golfed in the respective men's and women's leagues. They also used to play in the monthly "nine and dine" event, which they really liked, as well as still occasionally playing together. My father had always been a good golfer, but after he retired and had more time to work on his game, he got even better. By contrast, my mother was not a natural athlete and it took many years for her to develop a solid and consistent game. It is so unfortunate that just as she was finally really starting to hit her stride as a golfer, a major health crisis stopped her from ever playing again.

- ☒ July 25, 1991 – Although my handicap is 14, they have lowered it to 8 because of all the prizes that I have won.

- ☒ August 10, 1994 - Marg phoned to tell me that she tied Sheila Fallis but Sheila conceded. Marg now plays the Club Class-A champion, Sue Holton.

- ☒ August 13, 1994 – Marg left to play Sue Holton for the club match play championship. Marg phoned at 4pm. Apparently Sue Holton beat her after 27 holes.

- ☒ September 6, 1994 – Marg golfed in the Tuesday ladies' at Irish Hills and had a sparkling 49-50. She also won the ladies' draw.

My father retired on March 13, 1987. My parents immediately left for their first prolonged stay in Florida. Seven days later, they bought a mobile home in Titusville, Florida, where many fellow Canadians also owned mobile homes. True to form, one of the first things my father did was buy grapefruit trees to plant beside their new mobile home. He continued to add to his mini orchard over the years, eventually growing a white and red grapefruit tree, as well as an orange and tangerine tree. He even trained one of the permanent residents of the mobile home park to apply additional fertilizer during the nine months he wasn't there.

- ☒ March 24, 1987 – Bought two grapefruit trees (Ruby Red).

- ☒ February 21, 1991 – There was one open flower on the Marsh grapefruit, the first few leaf buds on the Ruby Red and very few small leaf buds on the Valencia Orange. There were many new buds on the Davey tangerine that had most of its new growth killed by the recent frost.

I was curious about the name Marsh grapefruit. My father explains, "It is the name for the grapefruit with the white pulp. The Ruby Red, with red pulp, is a variety derived from Marsh Grapefruit. Many people prefer it. All the white grapefruit at the grocery store are Marsh grapefruit."

After that first winter, my parents would leave for Florida just after New Year's Day and return for Easter each year. This three-month stay became their regular pattern. While many of their fellow snowbirds spent the day in their sunrooms or visiting Florida's famous theme parks, my parents preferred spending their time searching out nature trails and undeveloped beaches. One of the great benefits of Titusville was the presence of NASA's Kennedy Space Center. NASA owns huge tracts of land around the space centre. These lands are mostly in a natural state, including oceanfront beach areas. Between infrequent launches, these natural areas are open for the public to enjoy. My parents certainly made full use of exploring them.

Ever the botanist, my father started to collect a small library of books on the local flora and fauna of Florida. Within a couple of years, he became very knowledgeable about them. My parents even became Friends of the Enchanted Forest, which at the start of their time in Florida, was a low-key natural area on the outskirts of Titusville. This area of virgin forest contains many species that are otherwise extinct in Florida. They used to go there quite often to walk the trails. Over time, it has become a more developed attraction, including a huge pavilion structure.

⌗ January 16, 1988 – I drove along the wildlife trail back of the beach and saw two alligators, two wild pigs, and many birds.

⌗ March 22, 1988 – We left for the Fairchild Botanic Garden in Miami at 6:15 am and saw a Florida panther leaping across Hwy. 85 just south of Titusville. We arrived south of Miami about 11 am and spent over 2 hours in the garden.

⌗ April 1, 1989 – We drove to New Smyrna Beach and the

Turtle Mounds.

- January 11, 1990 – We went to Playalinda and walked on the beach and along the nature trail afterwards. There were more birds but not nearly as many as two years ago. Most of the vegetation was dead from the pre-Christmas freeze. We saw nine alligators.

- February 17, 1991 – We went for a long walk on the beach. A space vehicle was on the pad but the beach was open. We saw many birds and our first armadillo of the year.

I have never known my parents to be as socially connected as when they were in Florida. There were frequent parties, bingo, golfing, and daytrips. Initially my parents spent a lot of their time with other Canadians, but as time went on, they developed good friendships with many of the American snowbirds and permanent mobile park residents.

About once or twice a week, my father would golf in the morning and go shrimping in the evening. Most of the shrimpers were locals or people who came from Orlando. Their friends in the mobile park used to say to him, "You go down there at night. Aren't you afraid?" He wasn't. He knew everyone. When he arrived, they would greet him with, "Here comes Canada!"

Sometimes when he went shrimping, no one would catch anything. "The old joke was, shrimping when the shrimp aren't running is like trying to watch paint dry. It was boring," he says. But my father used to enjoy it whether they were running or not. The pier was located on the Indian River estuary, providing a lot of interesting wildlife to see, especially dolphins and manatees. My father comments, "There were also always a lot of people walking on the pier at night, both locals and visitors from all over the United States. Visitors would ask what they were doing. The shrimpers were more than happy to explain it to them. You always had people to talk to. Sometimes the shrimp ran so much that your arms got tired scooping them up in the net." There was one guy, Little Joe, who shrimped every night. He caught lots of shrimp, which he sold. One time my father asked him, "Joe, you're here every night. What's the secret to make sure you are here when the shrimp are running?" He replied, "The secret is ... be here every night."

- March 24, 1989 – I shrimped after supper. There were only 4 shrimp caught on the whole pier when I left at 9:10 pm.

- January 10, 1990 – I went shrimping with Ernie. I caught 5 and Ernie 4. It was a beautiful night with many dolphins passing by.

- February 9, 1990 – I went shrimping after supper. The pier was packed when I arrived. I could only set up on the east end, near a breaker. I caught 120 between 7:15 and 9:15 pm.

- February 13, 1990 – Marg and I cooked and prepared 183 shrimp that I had caught.

- January 8, 1991 – I put in my light at the pier, came home for supper and was back shortly after 6 pm. I caught 30 by 8:50 pm on a windy day, working off the south side. The shrimp were very skittish and hard to catch.

- January 14, 1991 – I put in my light at the pier at 5 pm. I saw a manatee. I caught 16 shrimp, all before 7:30 pm. I saw two more manatees and two dolphins.

- February 18, 1991 – I went with Ernie and put my light in and later shrimped. I caught 44 and Ernie far more. They were running deep and there were a lot of floating weeds at my site.

To attract the shrimp, each person hung a light off the pier. There were electric outlets on the pier. You paid a couple of dollars for the use of an outlet. Some nights there were relatively few people when the shrimp started running. However, my father quickly found out that within a half an hour the pier would be packed with people. The people that made their money from the outlet charge on the pier made sure to get the word out when the shrimp were running. They had a list of telephone numbers and would phone everyone to alert them.

Unfortunately, eventually the municipal pier rotted and then hurricanes damaged it to the point where it was condemned. They wouldn't allow people to use it. The local government kept saying they were going to allocate the funds to repair the pier. When the pier closed, my father went out four or five times with one of his neighbours who owned a party boat. Some people hung lanterns from a bridge so they could shrimp. This was too dangerous for my father's taste. They finally built a new pier a few years ago in conjunction with a new bridge. When asked if he will return to shrimping off the new pier, my father says he would like to if he gets the opportunity. Unfortunately, to date the opportunity has not presented itself and now that my parents rarely travel to Florida, or anywhere else, it is not likely to.

25
STROKE SURVIVORS

On June 15, 1995, the golden years of my parents' retirement ended abruptly. On that day, my sixty-four year old mother took a nap after lunch. That my fit and active mother was taking a nap should have been a warning sign in itself. I wish I had been more aware of what was going on. During her nap, my mother suffered a major stroke. When she awoke, she didn't know that half her body was paralyzed. She tried to get up. This effort launched her off the bed and onto the floor. She lay there in a semi-conscious state for several hours, until my father came home.

✍ June 15, 1995 – I arrived home from golf about 3:30 pm. Marg was on the floor between the bed and the window. She appeared paralyzed. She also had a severe knock on the side of the head from obviously hitting her head on the end table. We all arrived at the hospital shortly after the 911 ambulance. Marg had a major stroke and the prognosis was poor.

On that day, my mother suffered a devastating stroke, which we later learned in medical parlance, was termed a "right cerebrovascular accident resulting in a left hemiplegia." It is amazing how quickly you become entrenched in the medical details of a close family member's health problems. The stroke resulted from questionable treatment she had been receiving for an irregular heartbeat. My mother's young age and healthy lifestyle were without doubt the reasons she survived such a massive stroke. As it was, the left side of her body was partially paralyzed, with the worst damage to her left arm. As a lefty, this was particularly destructive and challenging.

The lead up to and after effects of my mother's stroke provide an unfortunate illustration of the progress of this devastating bodily trauma. There were warning signs, fainting and weak spells, up to five years before that fateful day. The rigour and attention of the medical industry was not what it should have been. My mother's propensity "not to want to bother people" was also a factor that did not help in the equation.

In 1991, she had been diagnosed with an irregular heartbeat and told that it would get worse as she got older.

☢ December 13, 1994 – Marg went to her doctor. Marg's irregular heartbeat seems to have stabilized. She was given a prescription for 3 months medication, told to take one aspirin a day and was told that her doctor would arrange an appointment with a heart specialist for a time after mid-April 1995.

My mother's health continued to worsen, with more fainting spells and an increasing routine of afternoon naps. A little over a week before her stroke, my mother finally saw a heart specialist.

☢ June 8, 1995 – Marg went to her heart specialist and he confirmed that she has an irregular heartbeat and there is danger of a stroke unless she got things stabilized. He gave her two kinds of medicine and she is not to drive until she gets her medicine stabilized.

☢ June 9, 1995 – Marg felt a little woozy with her new medication.

☢ June 11, 1995 – Marg seems to be having a reaction from her heart medicine.

I purposely called this chapter Stroke Survivors, because this milestone event plunged both of my parents' lives into turmoil as they struggled to deal with a completely new reality.

For my mother, the active independent lifestyle that had been her life, ceased on that day. After being subjected to two months of hospital care, three months in a rehabilitation therapy facility, and eight months of outpatient rehabilitation therapy, formal health support ended. In the end, her level of recovery would not have allowed her to live on her own. Almost all the activities my mother had previously enjoyed — cooking, knitting, walking, golfing, canoeing, skating, and cross-country skiing — were no longer options for her. The only two activities that she has been able to continue to enjoy are reading and playing bridge. The main household task that my mother has consistently been able to perform is washing the dishes. She rarely used the dishwasher before the stroke and this did not change afterwards. It is a point of pride that she is able to contribute to the household chores in this small way.

After her stroke, my mother was embarrassed about her physical disabilities in public places. Her contemporaries were still fit and active in their sixties and by comparison she saw herself as diminished. She has never wanted to walk, even short distances, with her quad-cane in public. Her timid nature certainly acerbated this. However, as time went on and her contemporaries aged and developed their own infirmities, this gap narrowed. In fact, many of the people that were healthy at the time of my mother's stroke are now deceased. I have also found that my mother thinks of herself as a different person since her stroke. She will occasionally make a comment that refers to the pre-stroke person she was as dead. She mourned the loss of the person she had been.

For my father, aside from the constant worry, the stroke meant at the age of sixty-seven taking on a new role as caregiver. Dad recounts, "This changed everything in both of our lives.

Overnight, I had to learn how to cook and do the laundry. My oldest son, Don, who had flown in from Calgary and was staying with me, was the one who gave me my first lesson on using the washing machine. I found this hard at first, especially in addition to handling all the trauma of dealing with the new reality of a partially paralyzed wife. However, as time passed, it all became easier."

For almost a year, my mother was in the hospital or rehabilitation centre. When she was in the hospital, my father was in to see her very early each morning. My father says, "Many times she would not receive her breakfast until 8:30 a.m. I did most of the work in getting her ready for the day and in getting her breakfast. I came to know where the refrigerator was and would organize juice, yogurt, and toast each morning and then bring it to Marg. The nurses came to depend on me doing this work, so they could attend to other patients." For his own meals, Dad would eat in the hospital cafeteria. He always requested the same thing, a hamburger. It got to the stage where as soon as my father would walk into the cafeteria, someone would shout, "Get the burger ready!"

Once my mother returned home, my father became her full-time caregiver. Since then, he does virtually everything around the home. "I'm no chef," he says, "but I've become a competent cook of the basics. I'm not starving and neither is Marg. Most of the time, it doesn't bother me to be the caregiver. It is something I have come to accept. I have always been the type of person to accept what comes my way and to do the best I can with it. I just do whatever needs to be done and get on with things. This trait has saved me a lot of anguish."

My father comments, "People will say to me, how come you have been able to look after your wife for nineteen years? With periodic exceptions, I get personal satisfaction from doing it. Some of what I have to do for my wife is pretty darn awful, but I do it, and get satisfaction from helping her. I like having a nice clean house. I like helping with the dishes." That said, the effort of caregiving has periodically taken a toll on my father. The first time was at the seven-year mark. I could see that things were out of control, but was unable to see how to help my father. In desperation, I found an eldercare consultant. My brother, Steve, and I went to see her. She provided us with information, the most interesting of which was that seven years is a recognized threshold for caregiver burnout. Passing on this information alone was hugely helpful to my father in moving forward. The information validated and gave expression to how he was feeling. This also highlighted for me the need for even more rigorous attention to ensuring my father had time for himself. Right from the beginning, at various times, my father had wanted to give up his research and golfing to concentrate fully on taking care of my mother. My brothers and I consistently encouraged him to keep doing the things that gave him so much pleasure. I am so glad we did. I would say that these outside interests have been, and continue to be, instrumental in his ability to cope as well as he has for so many years.

As both of my parents have aged, it has become increasingly difficult for them to cope. In addition to the effects of the stroke, the natural aging process made it more and more difficult for my mother to function, especially coupled with other health problems. Similarly, as my father aged, his ability to cope with caring for my mother became increasingly challenging. Over the years, my father has had several crises, both emotional and physical, which necessitated the need for my mother to go for a week or a month into a seniors' care facility to allow him to have a period of respite from caring for her. For almost a decade, my father has suffered from an undiagnosed chronic pain. His doctor has repeatedly told him that he believes the cause is related to the stress of caregiving.

One of the interesting benefits of my mother's time in these care facilities was seeing how much she enjoyed the social activities available to her. When she was first released from hospital after the stroke, I had tried to interest her in some type of outside social activity. At that time, she wasn't ready, but her exposure to this increased social interaction put her in a better frame of mind to respond positively to a new suggestion that I look for a day program. The challenge was finding a program that would be of interest to my mother but not place further demands on my father. I found such a program at the Abbottsford Centre. Twice a week they would pick my mother up and drop her off again, after providing a program of any number of activities. Really, I think what my mother enjoyed the most was just interacting with a consistent group of people: the bus driver, the other program participants, and the staff at the Centre. It improved her quality of life and had the added advantage of providing two days per week when my father could pursue his own interests in a worry-free way.

There are countless entries in my father's diaries that chronicle the progress of this traumatic time for our family. While my father has said that writing in his diary has never been therapeutic for him, I think that during this time, it certainly was.

✍ June 17, 1995 – I awoke early, at 5 am, to a bleak morning without Marg. How I miss her!

In my opinion, the chronic lack of communication, coordination, and monitoring of patients is at the core of problems in the health care industry in Canada. I'm a project manager. I manage projects that largely involve inanimate objects. My industry recognizes that the constant hand-over of a project from one manager to another is inefficient and greatly increases the chance of problems. If my industry performed like the health care industry, there would be chaos. This lack of consistent attention to patients is found at all levels in the health care system. Where did this concept of having a different nurse every day come from? Nurses are in the best position to know and address the needs of their patients. Lack of coordination leads patients to be subjected to repeated tests because the results are not shared well within the system. Not only is this costly, but it means patients must tolerate often undignified and painful tests more than once, all because the system is so inefficient.

The system is focused on itself, not the patient. Repeatedly I have seen the patient's needs being put at the very bottom of the list, and sometimes I don't even think they are on the list. It makes no sense to wake up a patient who has finally fallen asleep after an upsetting and trying day in order to take a non-emergency health reading. Uninterrupted sleep is the best healer. You would think that if anyone understood this, it would be health care practitioners.

Finally, I have repeatedly observed the lack of recognition and respect that the caregiver is given within the health care system. Well-meaning social workers will often focus totally on the needs of the person who has suffered the stroke, to the exclusion of the caregiver. In reality, the caregiver is usually taking the full brunt of handling the work and stress of the day-to-day needs of the stroke patient. I have had to intervene on a number of occasions when well-meaning attempts to provide support have in fact made the situation worse by providing assistance counter to the needs and wants of the person actually doing all the work, the caregiver. In recent years, as my mother's health problems have become more diversified and complex, and I see my father increasingly struggling to cope, I have suggested that perhaps it is time for them to consider placing my mother in a long-term care facility. Ever the caring and determined person that he is, my father's response was, "I have thought about it, but as far as I am concerned, we sink or swim together." What can you say to that?

PHOTOGRAPHS

1952: Margaret McDonald and Gerry Mulligan at graduation from Macdonald College

1963: Fieldtrip (Mulligan and Crompton), seasonal high country road through Kananaskis from Coleman to Banff

1968: Gerry Mulligan on fieldtrip to Mt. Rowe, Waterton National Park, collecting *Draba*

1969: Family fieldtrip to collect *Draba*, Margaret, Steve, Don, Julie and Paul on top of Sunshine, Banff National Park

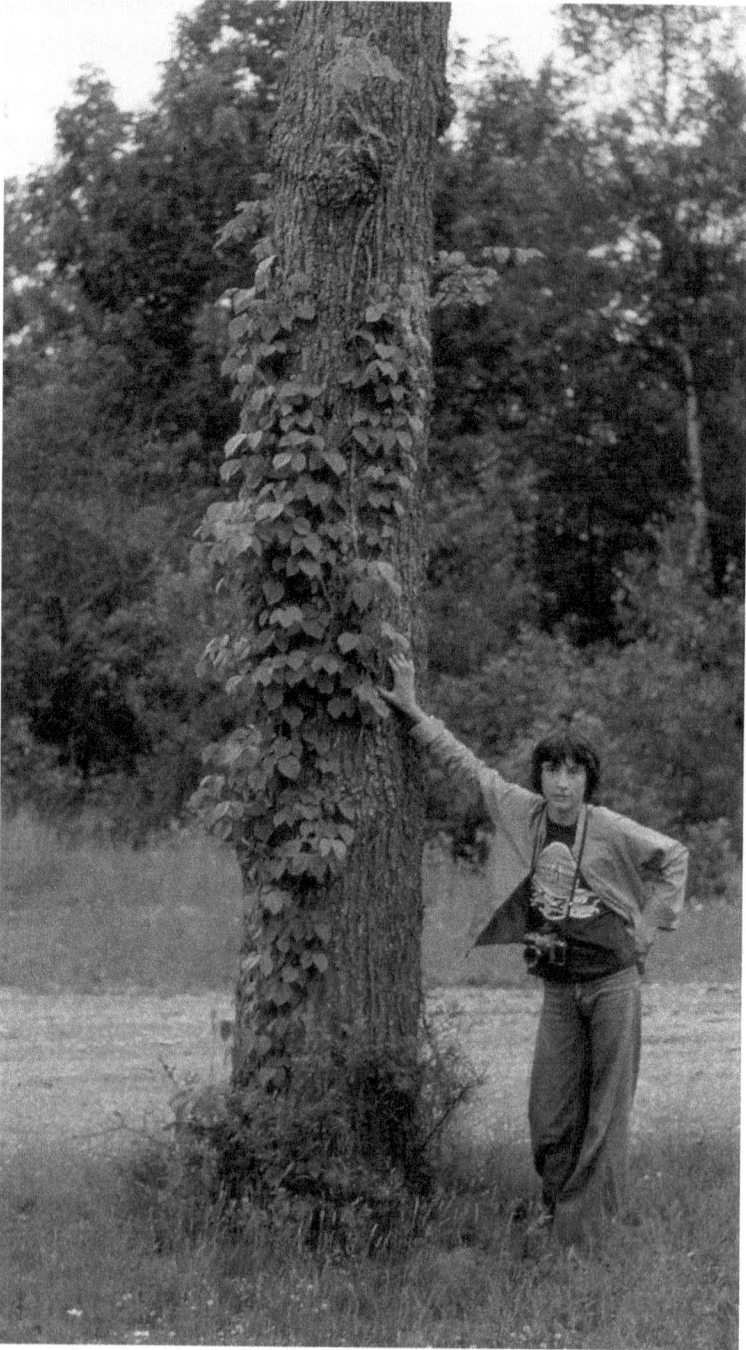

1978: *Rhus* fieldtrip to Boston area, Paul standing beside hydro pole covered in climbing poison ivy

2014: Entire family celebrating Margaret and Gerry's 60th wedding anniversary on a weekend trip to Mt. Tremblant, Quebec

ABOUT THE AUTHOR

Julie Mulligan is the second oldest of the four children of Gerald and Margaret Mulligan, and their only daughter. She is a landscape architect and biologist. She worked for twenty-one years as a consulting landscape architect in the private sector. During this time, she was a branch manager with Project Planning Canada Limited and later acquired the Ottawa branch, to become principal of Mulligan & Associates, Ecosystem Planning and Design. In 2001, she sold the company and in 2002 made the initially difficult transition to the public sector as a project manager with the National Capital Commission in Ottawa. This is her first foray into the world of book writing. She is currently working on her second book, *Parks and Gardens of Ottawa.*

www.ingramcontent.com/pod-product-compliance
Lightning Source LLC
Chambersburg PA
CBHW060019100426
42740CB00010B/1534